Up From Tribulation

Based On A True Story

Written by Brigham Young's daughter
Susa Young Gates

Originally Published
in the
Juvenile Instructor
1890

Reprinted 1975, 2008

Table of Contents

About the Author

The following biographical information was primarily obtained from the LDS Biographical Encyclopedia, Encyclopedia of Mormonism, and the Utah State Archives.

"Up from Tribulation" was originally published in the *Juvenile Instructor.* It's author was identified only as Homespun, a pen name used by Susa Young Gates, a daughter of Brigham Young.

Susa was born on March 18, 1856, in Salt Lake City, the second daughter of Brigham Young and his twenty-second wife, Lucy Bigelow. From an early age, she displayed remarkable intellectual skills. She became well educated, first attending her father's private school where her curriculum included music and ballet. At age thirteen, she enrolled at the University of Deseret. She later attended Brigham Young Academy and Harvard University.

At the age of sixteen, Susa married Dr. Alma Bailey Dunford. Together they had two children. Dr. Dunford's alcoholism and her young age led to their divorce only five years later, in 1877, the same year Susa's beloved father passed away.

The year following, in 1878, Susa enrolled at Brigham Young Academy (later University) While a student there, she founded the departments of music and domestic science and conducted the school's choir. Susa was also a trustee for the University for forty years.

In 1879, Susa married her lifelong companion, Jacob F. Gates. Together they had eleven children. Altogether, Susa was the mother of ten sons and five daughters. Of her thirteen children, only five survived to maturity. Early in her marriage to Jacob, from 1885 to 1889, they served a mission to the Sandwich (Hawaiian) Islands.

After returning home to Utah, Susa became very involved with the woman's suffrage movement. She attended the International Council of Women in London. In 1899 she became the Chairman of the National Organization of Women's Press Committee, and with its leader, Susan B. Anthony, had tea with Queen Victoria on one occasion. She was the only U.S. delegate to the 1902 Copenhagen conference and was the official American delegate at the 1914 meeting in Rome. At one point, Susan B. Anthony offered Susa the post of secretary of the National Council of Women on the condition that she forsake Mormonism. Susa refused. Still, Susa was proud of her role in woman's rights and that she had been among the first women in the nation to vote.

Susa's activities, contributions, and service within the Church of Jesus Christ of Latter-day Saints were no less impressive. She served in the General Board of Young Ladies Mutual Improvement Association from 1889 to 1911 and in the Relief Society General Board from 1911 to 1922. Susa also had a great passion for genealogy and temple work and did a great deal of work on her father's ancestry. She wrote the Church's first manual on genealogy and was head of research at the Utah Genealogical Society. She also served as an ordinance worker in the temples at St. George and Salt Lake City. She was a close friend of third Church President Wilford Woodruff and of other church leaders. Because of her prominence within the Church, she was once referred to as the thirteenth apostle.

When Susa was young, she was directed by her father to strengthen the youth through writing. In that endeavor, she became co-editor of the University of Deseret's *College Lantern*, possibly the first western college newspaper, and later founded both the *Young Woman's Journal* and the *Relief Society Magazine*, the latter which she edited. Her literary skills led to her being called by one biographer, "the most versatile and prolific LDS writer to ever take up the pen in defense of her religion." Besides writing biographies, histories, articles and plays, she also wrote several fictional novels, such as *John Steven's Courtship* and *The Prince of Ur.* Just two years before her death, she published a biography of her father, *The Life Story of Brigham Young*.

Susa Young Gates died on May 27, 1933, at the age of seventy-seven.

Susa defended plural marriage throughout her life although research has not shown that she ever lived that law. Interestingly, in 1920 she acted in a proxy temple marriage sealing on behalf of Lydia Mamreoff von Finkelstein Mountford and President Wilford Woodruff, who were both then deceased. This sealing may be significant because some historians indicate the possibility that Mountford may have married Woodruff as a post-manifesto plural wife before his death in 1898. Regardless of their relationship while living, Susa's role in the proxy sealing of her friend, the former Church president who had been a polygamist, to yet another wife suggests her perception of the importance of plural marriage as a law of God.

Susa explicitly stated some of her views about plural marriage in two articles that appeared in Church publications. The first, "A childless wife like Sarah," was published in the Women's Exponent in 1898. The second was her editorial, "Why was the Manifesto issued?" in the Young Women's Journal. These are reprinted over the next few pages.

A Childless Wife Like Sarah

Long ago in the lovely vales of Utah, dwelt a childless married woman. After seven years of unsatisfied longing, loving and reverencing her worthy husband more as the years proved him of the highest type of manhood combined with great integrity, they both greatly desired offspring which it seemed in vain to hope for.

At last, with full consent of all concerned, this worthy man took to wife another Daughter of Zion, familiarly known and loved by both husband and wife. In a year's time a son was born to gladden their hearts and in due time another son, then a daughter, then another son.

Then after nearly a score of years of waiting, a son previously named and promised by the spirit of prophecy, came to the childless wife. She was visited by hundreds of women, rejoicing that she had triumphed and saying she had been blessed even as Sarah of old, she herself knowing it was even so. And with such foundation they felt they must not fail. ... Their greatest ambition being to prove worthy to live in this most holy and revealed family order, with the father of their offspring throughout a never ending eternity.

The writer having been born through this same order of marriage, her father one of the first apostles in the Church, cannot do otherwise than revere the same. ... With her belief and remembering her pioneer parents, feeling a divine assurance that these conditions will exist forever in eternity for the faithful, she naturally enters a plea for the principle as a souvenir for her children, this pure and holy order born in.

- — -

Why was the Manifesto issued?

I am about to take a position in answering this important question which I feel sure will incite ninety-nine out of every hundred women who will read this with a feeling of strong denial. But my hundred sisters, one and all, if I am right in my position, no amount of opposition on your part will make me wrong. There has been a good deal said about this question, and yet I think some of the most important things have not yet been uttered by anyone. Granted that this nation bears the heavy burden of responsibility in regard to this matter which we all readily acknowledge, yet there remains the fact that those who live in Zion and who are usually called Saints will surely have to render an account which is their own. Well all know there are two sides to every question, and rarely is it that a wrong is done, especially in the nature of a curtailing of vested rights and privileges, whether in the family or in the nation, where each party is not more or less to blame. We have not injured the United States, but we have, I solemnly believe, so weakened the power of the Spirit in our midst by our own acts, that that mighty Spirit was not able to help us as we might have wished. No, I suppose most of you, my women readers, will say, as I have heard multitudes of women say in the last two years, "Well, I know who is to blame; the men have not dealt righteously with their wives, and have sought their own selfish pleasure instead of the feelings of their wives." I love truth too well that I shall allow you to say, and I agree with you in saying, that in some and perhaps in too many instances, this has been the case. Granted, then, that the men have been at fault in the matter of not being sufficiently unselfish. Granted also, without argument, that some men did not properly appreciate this glorious principle, and have neglected and slighted their opportunities. But, my dear and always loved sisters, I have a serious charge to bring against you and against myself in this matter, and I ask your kind and indulgent attention. To begin with, don't say that I am not in a position to talk on this matter, because of my not having had the privilege of entering into that order. Right is right, and principle is principle, whether it is spoken by an old maid or a woman in polygamy. Therefore, I ask you to listen and then prayerfully ask yourselves if I have spoken by the divine Spirit of Truth or by some false and delusive spirit. I say in all sad frankness that we, the women of the Church of Jesus Christ of Latter-day Saints, have a grievous sin to answer for in that we have too many of us treated this sacred and holy principle with neglect, sneers, mocking abuse and even cursing and railing. Is that so? Do you know of any women who have said they would never consent to marry a man who had another wife? Do you know of any women who have said they would not marry a man who would not promise them never to go into that order? Do you know of any women who have put every conceivable block in the way of their husband entering into that order? Do you know of any women who have tortured their husbands almost to death of the Spirit by their cruel and unjust complaints, uttered in season and out of season, in private and in public? Do you know of any women who have thought only of themselves, have worked only for themselves, have wept only for themselves, have prayed only for themselves? Do you know of any woman who has brought up her tender children in an atmosphere of loud and bitter complaint against their father, and against his every act? Do you know of any women who have insidiously taught their children to hate the principle that gave them birth? Do you know of any woman who has said openly or privately that not one of her daughters should enter into that order with her consent? Do you know of any women who have said they would rather see their children dead than in that order? Do you know of any women who openly rejoiced when the Manifesto was issued, and who held many and joyous jubilees with their daughters over the prospect? Do you know of any women who have demanded the last farthing from their husbands and denied the right of other women who were his wives to one cent? Do you know of any women who say or feel that their husbands have never suffered one trial in this order? Ask all these questions, and then I can leave you to answer them all, and I will venture to say that the answers will lead you to some startling conclusions. Talk about the sufferings in that order being borne by women only?

I thank God and one woman for the revelation I had on that subject. I have often had her words quoted to me, and I quote them again. Said she: "A woman don't have half the trouble in plurality that a man does. Why, she has only herself to please, and he has two or a dozen as the case may be." Her words came like a flash of light to me, and since then God has given me experiences which have fastened that truth upon my mind with never-ending power. Don't tell me all the suffering of that order and the terrible sufferings caused by the separations made necessary by the Manifesto have been endured by women. I wouldn't be a man and try to bear the burdens and trials he must needs bear, if a he has any conscience in his bosom, in living that order for all this world could give. One man told me in simple burning words something of his trials, both before and since the Manifesto. Of how he struggled with two selfish and determined women, each determined to claim him and all he had, and each with families of growing children. Of how he had crept out some nights into his cornfield, and in the agony of his soul had torn up the ground with his nails to relieve the pain at his heart. Did he love them both? With the devotion of a lover, else he would not have suffered so keenly. "Why," said Apostle Moses Thatcher to me once, in talking upon this subject, "do you think Abraham suffered most because of his own pain, or because he saw the pain he was inflicting upon his only son? Do you, as a mother," he continued, "not see the day when you would give your very life to spare pain and the pangs of death to the beloved child who is dying before your eyes? Which is the greatest suffering, to bear the pain yourself, or see the one you love best on earth bearing a pain, and for your sake, too, a pain which you cannot prevent, and which you can only witness and suffer in longing, awful sympathy." That was another revelation to me. And then let me ask how many of our sisters have sat idly by and allowed their husbands to waste the precious opportunity that is now taken away, and they have simply let the matter go on, inwardly rejoiced that their heart strings were not going to be tested. Do you know, have you ever read, what Christ said? If you are not willing to leave father and mother, houses and lands, you are not worthy of Him. We are not asked to leave our husbands, but only to test our devotion to God and His kingdom, or whether we love man and our own ease best. Sisters, I stand appalled at the magnitude of my sin and yours!

Explanatory Notes

This story, based on the lives of true characters, was originally published as a series in the *Juvenile Instructor* in the year 1890. The *Instructor* was an official Church publication, which was "Designed Expressly for the Education and Elevation of the Youth."

The author apparently worked on developing *Up From Tribulation* into a novel titled, "His Three Wives," but the manuscript – which appears complete – was never published. Perhaps the subject matter was considered too controversial after the Manifesto of 1890 officially banned plural marriage in the Church.

Several words (*gay* and *nigger*, for instance) have changed meaning in common usage since this story was first written, but the text remains unaltered to maintain the authentic voice of the writer and to accurately reflect the language used at the time it was written.

Part I

"Don't go out tonight, Willard."

"Why not, Pussy?"

"Because, because – promise me, Willard, not to go out tonight."

"All right, I promise. On my knees? Is that necessary?" taking the girlish form in his arms he continued, "Of course I will not go out if you feel so keenly about the matter.

"Oh, Willard, do you love me?"

"Well to anyone with eyes for anyone with genuine American ears, that question seems somewhat superfluous. What does this look like, anyway?" holding her as he spoke, close, close to his heart. So close indeed that her breath stopped. When she was once more released, she whispered,

"But tell me, dear –"

"You tell me! Do you love me? With your whole heart and soul? Would you now, could you, dear, sacrifice everything earthly for me?

"What a foolish question," evaded she. "Am I not your wife?"

"That is exactly the reason I asked. You are my wife, and as such should be willing to follow through prosperity and through adversity, through sickness and through health, through good and through evil report, aye even unto death," he spoke with peculiar emphasis, and raised her face in his two hands that he might look down through her eyes into her very soul.

"Willard, you scare me almost. But let me ask you a question. Ought not you to love me equally well, clinging to me even until death?"

"Yes, pet I ought. And once more remembering my marriage vows I solemnly promise to be true to you through every changing scene until death. Come now, this is enough of sentiment, give me some supper, little woman. If you knew the amount of work I have done today, you would certainly lay an extra slice of bread on the plate."

Away flew the young wife, hurrying her delayed preparations and singing as she went, forgetting at the time all her fears and cares.

"Where is the evening paper, Patsey?" The pet name he had given her when first married came far easier to his tongue than her own stately name, Hortense.

She stopped suddenly, colored and stammered as she replied that she hardly knew, it was somewhere around.

The young man looked somewhat surprised and with a quickly suppressed whistle he sprang up and after diligent search found the paper in question directly under Patsey's workbasket.

This fact seemed to sharpen his wits and his eyes for almost with the first glance he read:

> "Those infamous Mormons will hold another meeting tonight in the Barton Hall, thus seeking to convert and corrupt (interchangeable terms in this case) every young woman in this town. Let parents beware, and watch the very movement of their young charges, while this disreputable crowd is in our midst."

The young man looked up sharply. Hortense was quietly, so quietly now, putting on his supper, pouring out the tea with a sort of trembling quiet.

Whatever his thoughts, he said nothing but gravely drew his chair to the table and began his meal.

"Have you been home all day?" he asked at last.

"No dear, I ran over to Aunt Mildred's a little while this afternoon, and do you believe it, she gave me three quarts of her delicious damson jelly. I helped her, and so she insisted on my bringing nearly half of it home. She is so kind, Willard. And do you know," she rattled on nervously, "she gave me some pretty strong hints about my Christmas present from her being a grand piano. Wouldn't that be too lovely?"

"Yes, dear, perfectly jolly. What else were you and aunt talking about?"

"Oh, everything! Jenny Birdeye is going to be married to Harry Everett this fall, and just imagine, we are going to begin the Barton Sociables again this very month. And now you know we are married, and we can take our own turn having it at our house; won't that be nice? And such cakes as I shall cook! Only one solid, and one liquid, that's the rule for refreshments, you know."

Willard Gibbs pushed away his plate at last, and with a faint sigh he went to his flute and began playing in a soft, sad undertone a sort of running accompaniment to his gloomy thoughts and half-defined fears.

The house was speedily set to rights and then the young husband and wife, only four months wedded, sat down in the neat little sitting room, she with her bit of sewing, he with his flute.

The small lamp on the table shed a soft quiet light over the girl's face and showed to the watchful eyes of her lover-husband opposite every line and curve in the lovely face and head.

For Hortense Randolph was a lovely girl. Rather tall, well made in every way, her proud head sat on her shoulders with a pretty grace all its own. Oval cheeked, ruby lipped, and dark eyed was she with the delicate regular features nature gives to few of her chosen ones. Her hair hung far below her waist, and if it was perfectly straight it was fine and darkly abundant. She knew she was beautiful, she had always known it.

The Randolphs of Virginia were too well known to be at all modest in their own estimation. The branch of the family who had lived in and about Marysvale for three generations were only distantly related to famous John. Yet they were related, and counted with glowing pride to the common progenitor albeit going several generations back to do so.

Hortense had been left an orphan in early life, but her Aunt Mildred had very carefully reared her in all the well-established traditions of the family. Pride, love intense for anybody or anything with the magic name of Randolph, firm tenacity of will, even if this sometimes crushed down feeling and affection. Extreme kindness to everything inferior, provided always inferiority humbly confesses itself as such; sweet politeness to equals, quiet dignity to superiors, if such a race of beings could be found; a love for music and for the more solid parts of literature, such as history and the lesser scientific pursuits. All these were family traits, and were more or less firmly engrafted on the soul of the young orphan charge of Mrs. Samuel Randolph.

"Patsey," asked Willard, that evening, "how came you to choose me for a husband?"

"Why Will, what a boy thou art! Have you not asked that question a dozen times?"

"Yet it is not answered. Now just pitch right in, and tell it all, from first to last."

"Don't say pitch right in, Will; you know how I dislike such expressions."

"Well, well, go on."

"I don't know I am sure."

"Come here, Patsey. It is necessary, in order that this story may have due force, that you should sit close beside me. Very close, as it were. Here's my knee. Two knees. Item, knees, wife. Wife, knees. Wife, weight. Weight, exercise dormant. Exercise, digestion. Digestion, good nature. Implicit, it is necessary for you to sit on my knees if you wish to aid my digestion and secure to me my good nature. Hey, puss?"

15

Meanwhile the young girl had put aside her work, and with a quiet air taken her seat on the broad arm of his rocking chair.

"What made you fall in love with a careless, gay fellow like me without much money, and not any family records to boast of, you know."

Hortense turned around, took his face between her two hands, and looked long and with a growing passion of love and tenderness into the dark gray eyes.

The sweet moon of early wedded life was not yet at its wane, and both felt again the deep delicious thrill that such looks from eyes we love brings to man and maid.

He laid his head against her breast with a sweet sense of love and peace while he sat with her arms strained around his dear head as if to defy time or circumstance to rob her of him or his love.

At last she whispered.

"Will, Will love! Would you let anything on earth part us?"

"I will never willingly part with you, my wife, either in time or in all eternity."

"Say, Will, I want to ask you here, right here, while you are close to my heart: you won't let this terrible question of Mormonism come between us, will you?"

"No, dear, it shall not part us with my consent."

"Your consent, Willard, what do you mean?"

"What I say. I will never willingly part from you. Can you say the same, dear?"

"Well, what I mean is, you are not going to join such a terrible, vile, wicked people, and by such means cut yourself off from all your friends and family?"

"Patsey, I have been expecting something like this, more from the cruel taunts I have borne at the hands of your friends than from anything you have said to me. But now you have broached the subject, let us talk it out."

"You do love me?" questioningly, eagerly, sadly.

"Oh, Patsey, have mercy on me. Let us not drag our love into this discussion. Not now at least. I want to ask you, little woman, suppose I were to decide to move to South America or Russia and there build our home. Would you go with me?"

"Yes dear, willingly."

"You would? God bless the little heart, I did not believe it so true and firm. Now then, Patsey, I don't want to go to either of those distant or disagreeable places, but I want to go 'out west.' Out into that glorious country you and I have often talked glowingly about. Where men cease to be pygmies, ants in one reeking busy hive, but become great and free. Kings over the sweeping acres around them. Rulers over the dashing hordes of the plains. Potentates in a realm of immense peace and plenty. Here it is that I have selected to make our dear home, and here it is that my darling, true, loyal wife will gladly accompany me, will she not?"

And he stroked the soft, glossy head with the rough hand made gentle by love.

"Willard, I will go anywhere on earth with you, in honor. In honor, mind; I cannot consent to enter a life of disgrace, even with you. I want to ask you one question. Have you joined this disreputable set of Mormons?"

A pause. Then, looking up and into her eyes with sad firmness he answered, "Yes, I was baptized last Thursday by Elder Hayward."

"Oh, Willard," the young wife's eyes dilated as she looked, wider and yet wider. As the sense of it gradually came upon her, she gasped faintly, "Oh, how could you – do –" and she fell heavily against his breast in a groan.

This was the first but by no means the last scene of the same nature which occurred day after day for three weeks in the little cottage.

Willard Gibbs had quite as much firmness of character under his gay exterior as was possessed by his wife Hortense. He had accepted the gospel after a severe struggle with his own pride and his own desire for worldly comfort and ease. That he should meet opposition even from his wife he well knew. But he had received in his own heart a testimony of the truth of Mormonism as the "Work" was termed, and that divine testimony he was not disposed to lightly discard.

He had queried and questioned; and had been most solemnly promised that, if he would humble himself and go down into the waters of baptism receiving afterwards the imposition of hands for the reception of the Holy Ghost, he should assuredly receive a testimony from God as a result of this obedience to His law.

He had done so. And on his coming up out of the water, his soul had been lit up with tongues of flame, his whole being seemed filled with a radiant light, and he had broken forth into prophecy and thanksgiving.

Other testimonies had been added. Direct and most singular answers to his prayers had been given, and in answer to one of his fervent appeals, he was now strengthened and enabled to withstand all the fiery opposition brought to bear against him.

Yet, "Oh, my wife, " he would groan whenever the lovely image came up before his eyes.

They lived in a quiet little town of one of the Southern states, surrounded by friends and acquaintances who had known them from their infancy.

"Hortense," said Aunt Randolph, "if you allow one word of consent to fall from your lips in regard to this horrible plan, the disgrace of yourself and your husband shall lie forever at your door. Be firm, my dear, be firm."

"Aunty," they were sitting on the wide piazza of Mrs. Randolph's luxurious home, "do you know what it means to be firm? Look at the lovely setting sun. In what words could you persuade those tenderly quivering leaves that they must needs turn away their faces from the sweet glowing looks of the orb of the day? I love Willard. With my whole soul, with all of this weary, aching heart. Almost well enough to meet dishonor at his dear call."

"Hortense, you are talking without realizing the position you take. I have no doubt you love Willard. But if you love him, prove it. Dare you?"

"How Aunty?"

The lady threw her pet dog out of her lap, and leaning over her niece's low rocking chair she said in quiet tones, "Tell him, my dear, that he must choose between you and his crazy notion of going off with these Mormons."

"I can't, Aunt, oh I can't."

"Why can't you? You may be assured that this alternative will be all that is necessary to bring him to his senses. You know I never recommend anything which savors of divorce. No Randolph has ever so disgraced himself. But – even if worst comes to worst – it is a choice between two evils; and the evil of divorce I consider much less than to see you carried off to such a horrible, miserable life. But, my dear, cheer up. I don't think for a moment matters will come to such a pass as that. Only be firm. Remember always, you are a Randolph."

Hortense could not remain another moment at her aunt's, her mind was too full of surging passions.

Besides this strong argument of her aunt's she had determined to add a new, strange plea, whose very remembrance caused hot flushes of joy to swell in her heart till it leaped within her breast.

The sun had sunk below the rim of distant hills, and the faint white stars were beginning to dimple the face of evening. Around her the quiet evening sounds were filling the space; the frog croaked a serenade to his ladylove as he sat perched on a clump of leaves above the little pond. The crickets whistled and chirruped to one another the same old story of love and good fellowship. The gnats began to add their tiny burr to the evening hymn, and aloft in the trees the birds gave an occasional goodnight chirp.

Her road lay through a lane, with fields of waving cane on each side, and a marshy low border of stagnant water stretched on her right.

The loneliness of the hour and scene entered her being and seemed to add another element of jarring, contending emotions. She felt as if her whole soul were strung to a high pitch, and every chord would give answering sound of fulness, whether touched by love, hate or fear. Dimly she sensed that so firm was the undercurrent of her own willful, passionate being that whenever the chord might be that should be made to vibrate through her soul this night, its echoes would go on and on forever.

Her feet flew with eager swiftness over the path, for she knew her husband would be awaiting her return. Breathless, half frightened and nervous, she screamed out as she heard her name called out behind her.

"Why, pet," her husband said lovingly, "you ran so fast I could not catch up with you and so called. I am so sorry to frighten you. How you tremble."

"Do I? Yes, I think so. But do you know, Will, I was so anxious to get home and have a talk with you, and was so busy thinking I grew a little nervous."

"I came round by the road and got up to aunt's just five minutes after you left. So, Patsey, you've been up discussing the new piano? Have you decided on Steinway or Knabe?"

"We haven't talked of pianos, dear. But I want to ask you a question," with suspicious eagerness.

Fearing its nature, he replied, "Shall we not wait till we are home? You are trembling too much to talk; let us rather hurry homeward."

"No, Will," stopping in the path, "I must talk to you now, here. I want you, dear, to put your arms around me and let me say my say in your ear. But first answer me a question. You are not going to leave home?"

"Certainly not now, Patsey. Maybe not for years. So don't borrow any trouble about that, little woman."

"But I want to know more. Are you ever going out to Utah?"

"Don't Patsey; let that question alone. You don't understand anything about this matter, and prejudice would prompt all you might say. Forget this for a time."

"No, I shall not, cannot. Oh, Will, you don't know how I love you, nor how true and fond a wife I will be if you will only be true to me."

"What a queer little Patsey you are. Of course I'll be true to you. Could I ever be anything else?"

"Then, Will, I ask you, beg you to give up once and for all this awful thing called Mormonism for my sake, for your own wife's sake. Will you, dear?"

He had turned his head away and stood silently gazing on the marshy pool below, in which he saw mirrored faintly the sweet, innocent stars of night. A silent, agonized prayer went up from his wretched heart, for he saw it had come. Here was the one great battle to fight, to win. Alas! Only God could give him strength.

"Give up my heart's blood, my wife," he answered after a moment's pause. "You do not, cannot know what you ask. Let me ask a question. What do you mean, give up going to Utah? Is that what you mean?"

"Oh, yes, that and the religion, if such vile stuff could be called by so good a name, to give it all up."

"For your sake, for your dear sake, I will consent to give up all notion of going to the west, at least for many years. Now, dear, let this suffice. Come, let us go home."

"No, no, not yet. I must have it all out now, right now. Promise me you will have nothing more to do with any of them, not ever go to their meetings, nor anything. Oh, Will, surely it is nothing I ask compared to the sacrifices I would make for you."

He saw then it must needs be. So taking her hands in his own, he said firmly and so gravely, "Hortense, you ask me that which no man can or may do. You ask me to say in effect that the truth is a lie, and to deny the testimony of Jesus, my Master, which I have received. And although my very heart stops at the thought of hurting you so much, I must still answer, No, I will not, cannot deny my faith in the gospel nor separate myself from the Saints. Urge me no more. I will wait patiently, quietly till you can see this as it is, for months, years even, but I cannot become an apostate to what I know to be the truth."

And they stood thus silently looking into each other's eyes. Each saw – what? A firm, unshaken belief in and determination to maintain the rightfulness of their own position.

The girl did not faint nor cry out. Womanlike, the blow came gradually and just now she could not realize its force. Nor was she at the end of her reasoning and pleading; she still held her strongest reason, her most potent argument.

"Willard," she almost whispered, "bend your head close, listen, can you hear?" and she whispered a few, hurried, shy words in his ear.

"Is it possible?" he asked, and with a flood of joy and tenderness he pressed her close, so close to his heart. His wife, his dear little wife. The mother of his child.

Silently and rapturously they stood in each other's arms, the first sweet glimpse of that heaven wherein walk mothers and fathers joined by a baby's clinging hands opened wide and fair before their mental eyes.

"Now, Will dear, you will not, cannot leave me, can you?"

"Have I ever thought of leaving you, love; oh, believe it not."

"But, Will," and she drew back and put her hands on his shoulders to keep him a little away. "Understand me now clearly. You must choose, make your final and irrevocable choice between me and that monstrous sect. Oh, Will," with a little catch in her breath, for he did not answer, standing as if stunned by her words, "between, dear, between that and – and – us."

"What do you mean, Patsey?" he asked vaguely.

"What I say: you must give up this whole farce of religion or – yes, or me. I will not, cannot consent to link my name to such a vile, wicked scheme."

"Oh, you, you, Patsey, don't say such things to me. Here I am, see, dear," and he fell humbly on one knee down at her feet, "here I am at your feet to sue, to beg, I, your husband. Only be patient, wait a little, just a few months, and I will promise to quietly wait also, then we will bring this thing up and settle it. Not now, not tonight. Hear me, Hortense, dear wife."

His suffering, his seeming almost willingness to yield, his weakness and inability to look at such an alternative as that only strengthened the girl in her determination. If she waited –

"I will not wait! Now, here, tonight you must choose. Which shall it be, Willard, dearest, sweetest husband, come to my arms, I am –"

He arose, and once more, taking her two hands, said hoarsely, "Hortense, choose your words well. Do not trifle with me nor yourself. Have you weighed your words well?"

"Yes; I mean just what I say," she emphasized slowly.

"I know you too well to doubt it. Yet must I give you my decision. And understand, my wife, it can never, oh, help me heaven, never be anything else. I must be true to my Redeemer and His unpopular cause. Always know this, although I may be deserted by your love and sympathy, you can never, never in time or eternity get away from my love, my care."

"And you fling me aside? Throw my heart away for a new fancy? Oh, I cannot believe it."

"I have not thrown you aside, Hortense. Don't talk so wildly. Come home at once, you are ill and upset."

"Home? Let us at last understand one another. This is the end. You go your way, to vice and destruction; I, I return to my aunt's home, alone, disgraced." And for the first time tears gushed from her eyes.

Other arguments, pleadings and prayers followed.

"O my God," gasped the poor husband. "This is too much, it is more than I can bear; it will kill me."

"Shall I come with you?"

"Will you?"

"Gladly, if you choose me. Do you, Will?"

Like a voice at his ear came the words, falling on his torn and bleeding heart. "He that taketh not his cross and followeth after me, is not worthy of me."

A quiet calm came over him, and he turned to the anguished face of his wife and said, "God bless you, my wife, whatever choice you may make, whether you remain by your husband or return to your former home. My door is and always will be open to you wherever or whenever you will come. Remember that."

"You choose your vile Mormonism and leave me to my fate? So be it. Good night and goodbye forever."

Turning from him she sped like a wild thing back to her aunt's house.

"Aunty, O Aunty," she called; and for hours in her grief she sobbed, moaned, called her husband's name and even tore her hair and clothes. Her aunt left her to cry, knowing the first force must spend itself ere Hortense could be able to reason or listen to reason from anyone else.

One thing Mrs. Randolph was very determined about, and that was to strengthen her niece in her firm refusal to return to the home of her husband, unless Willard should "come to terms."

Poor Hortense! She had scarcely counted on such an ending to her plans. But she, too, was of firm, unyielding temperament, and in her mind prejudice and tradition formed as great a barrier against possible relenting as reason or right could have made.

The days passed heavily, the nights were long, restless torture. Yet she was firm. Gradually she steeled her heart to accept the change and to think of her husband as of one dead.

Part II

Great was the commotion in Marysvale when it was known that the "Mormons had robbed dear Hortense of her husband and home." Nobody stopped to reason on the matter, nothing was said on Willard's side of the question, not one voice was raised in his defense.

The great tide of gossip ebbed and flowed, now dying partially down and again augmented by some fresh supposed "development." In the height of it down came Mrs. Randolph's son Oscar from his business in Philadelphia. His pride, anger and prejudice were soon roused to the highest pitch, and he determined to seek out the insane husband and bring him to his senses or put the bullet of an outraged cousin in his heart.

Willard had remained at the little deserted home, perhaps with some faint hope that in time his young wife would relent and return. His parents' home was two miles out from Marysvale, and indeed, they too were so little in sympathy with their son that they felt it would perhaps bring him to his senses if his friends showed him by their actions how little sympathy he might expect from sensible people.

The day after Oscar's arrival was Saturday. Knowing Willard would be at his work in the day, he waited impatiently till evening should close in. Putting a couple of trusty pistols in his pockets, he at last reached the little cottage, one solitary light from the kitchen window showing it was occupied.

Willard answered the knock, and the two men stood for a moment looking keenly into each others' faces.

"Well, Willard, this is a devilish bad business," and, without invitation, he followed his host into the kitchen at the end of the hall.

Willard quietly pointed to the only vacant chair – the rest being taken up with dishes, clothing and sundry untidy articles. The whole place wore an air of quiet misery and desertion. The evening was chilly and in the rusty-looking stove a slow, uncheerful fire burned. In the middle of the room stood the table, one end cleared off and set with a bowl of milk and a plate of poor "pancakes," evidently baked that evening. The rest of the table was piled high with dishes and remnants of food. Everything was untidy and in the room was a faint, disagreeable odor that is always present where dirt and confusion reign.

Intent on his errand, Oscar scarcely saw the place, but stood by the table and poured, in one rapid flood, the invectives that had been gathering in his heart all the day long, closing with the words:

"You coward! To desert a woman who loves you as Hortense does! For what, too? A vile, beastly, rotten mess that decent men will not even speak of. Oh, you are a fine one to keep your marriage vows. What's the matter with you? Why don't you speak? Haven't you got anything to say? Has your deviltry robbed you of your speech?"

Willard had dropped his head into his hands and sat perfectly still during this fierce tirade.

With an oath Oscar threw a pistol on the table and demanded an immediate answer.

"Why don't you answer me? Good – man, you used to be quick enough to speak and brave as well. Have they worked some damnable spell upon you?"

Still no answer – not a breath. The silent, bowed figure seemed incapable of life or motion. Something in the profound quiet seemed to act like a sedative to the excited man, and instinctively his gaze wandered about him, absorbing the whole desolate scene. The misery of it all slowly quenched even his fiery anger.

"Willard," he said at last, quietly, "can't you speak to me?"

The head was raised, and on the pale, silent face were tears – a man's rare tears. The dark brown eyes were sad, mournful, pathetic; the firm mouth, with its passionate red lips, quivered with anguish, its violent trembling scarcely hid by the dark, silky mustache. The face was drawn with pain and sorrow, but not a trace of anger.

"Do you wish to talk to me, Oscar?"

"Why else have I come? Yet, to tell the whole truth, Will, I came to put a hole through you."

"Here am I," answered the man.

"O, I didn't come to shoot you down like a dog, only a duel. But you know I am the best shot and – . Well, no matter now; something here has made me feel queer."

How should he know that the silent figure had been filled with humble prayer to God?

"Now, old friend, let me talk a bit to you. Don't answer now, just listen. When you came to seek Cousin Hortense, I almost hated you. Yes, that's the short of it, and you need not look so surprised. I love Hortense," his voice low and deep in its quiet intensity, "but she don't love me – never will. Yet, Will, she is my one, my only love. And you – you, Willard Gibbs, won her love, married her, and now, for naught, you have flung her away!"

"Oscar, does this look as if I had deserted her, or she me? Old fellow, I am more wretched than tongue may tell. I have wandered in the vales of Paradise with my lovely bride, and now – now –" He got up on his feet and, with his arms flung above his head, paced to and fro in silent agony. After his grief was somewhat mastered, he sat down again and said, sadly: "Behold me, cast out of Paradise; not with my Eve by my side, but alone, alone. Man, man, can you not imagine something of what I suffer?"

The handsome face looked old and haggard.

"Listen, old friend; will you let me talk to you a little while? You are the first one who has ever visited me in my loneliness. I am a moral pariah, a spiritual leper – so my friends have decided. When you came tonight and I saw your pistol in your pocket, I bowed my head and asked God to let me die if it was His will, for I am weary of this life."

"Merciful heaven, Will, what has brought you to such a pass?"

"I met and conversed with two men who said they had been commissioned of God to preach His gospel. I told them such pretensions must necessarily be of the utmost worth or deserving of disgrace and exposure. They answered that they were ready with proof as strong as Holy Writ itself. I am not going to enter into an explanation of their particular doctrines and principles; enough now to tell you my story. Every tenet, every doctrine seemed, on thorough investigation, to be true – true as light and sunshine. I was told that if I complied with their law of baptism, in a spirit of humility, I should receive a divine testimony from God; even the Holy Ghost should visit me and I should know for myself and not for another that this was the truth. I did so, and, Oscar, I bear testimony to you tonight that this gospel is true, true as the Throne of Heaven itself," and, with a slow, strong emphasis, he brought his closed hand down upon the table, making the dishes ring.

"What a singular thing for man to say, or man to believe!"

"Aye, singular, indeed. Here am I, deserted by family, friends, and made an outcast from every society – even the lowest – alone, unable to resume my work, for no one will work where I am employed; my own workhands refuse to accept pay from me. Five months a bridegroom – and they have influenced my bride, my wife, whom I love better than my life, to leave me! What have I to look forward to – to hope for in this life? All this could be altered; would be changed, as it were, in the twinkling of an eye, if I would speak only two words – I retract. But hear me, Oscar; I can't do it – I can't. When my heart seems breaking for a sight of my dear wife's face, and I feel that one whisper would bring her back, the voice in my heart cries out, 'but it is true, and you will be false to Christ and His testimony if you say anything else'."

Once more he paced the floor to still the violence of his emotions.

"I am glad you have come, Oscar," he continued; "it has broken up the dead calm that seemed settling down over me, and you have roused me once more to thought, to action. Once more I will go out and seek work and thus crowd down this suffering in my heart."

"Well, old boy, I must confess I am sorry for you. I won't say that I think you are right, but at least you have got the courage of your convictions. I wish, though, you could see things different."

The men parted. The husband to resume his waiting for what he scarcely knew.

Oscar returned to his mother's home; and so decided was his defense of the "poor dupe" that his mother became alarmed, and an immediate journey for all three to a distant state was planned, ostensibly for the benefit of Hortense's health. Three days after the visit of Oscar, Willard saw a notice in the village paper of the departure of the Randolphs "on a long visit to a distant state."

She had gone, his dear little Patsey, without one word, one sign. It was almost too much for him to bear. Now, indeed, he knew for what he had waited – a faint hope that his wife would relent.

That night a chance traveling Elder came to his house, and to him Willard confided all his grief. The old man blessed him and comforted him. Together they read those holy passages in Matthew, Luke, and through the Apostles, proving that Saints in former days were tried – even all they could bear.

To Willard he gave this promise:

"Be of good cheer. Your God has not forsaken you. What has been taken from you, through your obedience, will be restored to you four-fold. Houses, lands, home, friends, family, wife and children. All shall be yours. Seek first the Kingdom of God and His righteousness and all other things shall be added unto you. Be faithful, be humble, and God will restore to you fourfold."

Within a month Willard had sold his home for a song (he could scarcely get rid of it, he was so despised) and had departed for the land of Zion in Utah.

Part III

Salt Lake City, Jan. 8th, 18 –
My Dear Friend Oscar:

The pictures which you so generously forwarded to me have just this moment been put into my hands. I cannot find words to express my gratitude to you. The face of my wife (she is mine still, and I shall always call her so) looks thin and sad. The child, hers and mind, our boy Harold, is lovely beyond description. O think of it, old friend, my own child, and I never have and mayhap never will see him!

I am glad to hear they are all pretty well and am likewise please that Hortense is once more getting strong and rugged.

You are very anxious to know how I am feeling and what I am doing. I am well in body and pretty well in mind. At times, a longing to be with my wife and boy seems to sweep over me, but generally I am quite contented.

The people here are simple and quiet in their habits, that is, the Mormons themselves, and all are very kind and good to me. To be sure, some of them don't act just as I think Saints should, but I am trying to separate people from principle in my mind, and not condemn the religion because of the sins of those who believe or pretend to believe in its teachings.

The Bishop of the –th Ward soon found me work in a small store where I am at present keeping books. I am so glad I took up bookkeeping while we were at —— College, for it is just now very convenient for me to be proficient in that study.

No, I have not fallen in love with any of the Mormon girls although there are some very pretty, nice girls here. I am quiet, reserved, unacquainted and unattractive. In truth I have taken little pains to be anything else.

Before I close I must tell you of the great happiness of my life. It is to go to meeting on the blessed Sabbath, and there hear prophets and apostles pour out a rich flood of truth and inspiration into our waiting hearts. This well pays me for all I have suffered and am at present undergoing. I wish I could impart some of this to you; but your request shall, for the present, be respected, and I 'will not preach Mormonism to you.' But I long to see and talk with you and humbly thank you for your kindness to me.

Write whenever you can or wish to, I am every longing to hear how all are.

Kiss my lovely boy for his absent father, and always think of me as

Your obliged and grateful friend,
"Willard Gibbs"

One year had passed since the young man had left his southern home; and too loyal was he to tell his friend of many little trials and troubles that had come upon him in an almost constant stream. These things had greatly tried his feelings, wounded him sometimes to the core, yet his faith in the gospel was as strong and as bright as when he first entered the waters of baptism. To his generous, impulsive, warm, southern blood, the cold, prudent, calculating habits and customs of this people, who were in the main, Yankees, were intensively selfish if not sordid. Prudence was another name in his ears for rapicity. A dollar in his pocket leaped out at the first hint of want or poverty, the first call for subscriptions. To see other men hesitate and count out a few cents with slow deliberation, asking Poverty if it could not earn its bread, was intolerable to the prodigal nature of the young man, and his spirit was chafed and galled at such associations.

He could not see the other side of the story; he little realized how slowly and painfully the money had come to his frugal companions. He had always had money, and always spent it freely. Not rich, his people were still comfortable, well-to-do, and in one word, they were Southerners.

Other trials also came. He was oftentimes misunderstood and misinterpreted. His whole-souled enthusiasm was called "gush," his anxiety "to help along" by word and deed was thought to hold a spirit of officiousness and self-conceit. He met with rebuffs on nearly every hand. Sometimes his soul felt sick and disgusted. At such times he would be tempted to remain at home on the Sabbath and read something distracting.

Not often did he give way; and what always seemed a strange thing, if he was feeling particularly sore on any one point, the speakers, or one of them, would say something especially adapted to his particular, taking up the contested point and so rounding it out into beauty and symmetry that the light of heaven shone through its transparent brilliancy.

Shortly after he had sent his letter to Oscar Randolph, a peculiar circumstance occurred.

He had taken lodgings in a house on Third South Street, a large house with furnished rooms to let. In the course of a few months he naturally became acquainted with a young man who occupied the room next to his own. From a bowing acquaintance sprung up a sort of intimacy. Willard found his fellow lodger a reader and student and many interesting tales were indulged in.

Gradually they took their dinners at the same restaurant, entered their rooms at the same hour, only to adjourn to the porch on pleasant evenings, and even stroll down in town together.

The stranger's name was the same as that of one of the leading men of the Church; and without questioning, Willard soon discovered that his companion was a distant relative of that great and good man.

Arthur Willis was rather below the medium height, grey eyes, light hair and not far from handsome. The expression of the eyes was mournful in the extreme and covered as they were with glasses, still strangely impressed the beholder. The lines about the mouth were hard, and betrayed a sarcastic temperament; yet his manner well controlled his evident sharpness.

The conversation often drifted into subjects of religion; and then, indeed, Willard could not conceal his surprise that such strange expressions should fall from his companion's lips. Tom Paine, Ingersoll and his master Voltaire were names frequently bandied between them.

In these conversations Willard never hesitated to express his views and would occasionally retort on Arthur for the strange views he seemed to entertain. This had continued for several months although Willard was becoming weary of repeated disagreeable discussions, and his hot blood began to resent the covert sneers at himself and ideas which Arthur scrupled not to throw quietly at him.

One day in the month of February, his employer called him into the back office and asked him to sit down.

"Brother Gibbs, do you take the T —— ?" he asked.

"No, sir," was the answer.

"You know the paper, I presume?"

"Yes, sir, I have heard it spoken of; and in fact, I have seen it several times in restaurants and such places."

"Brother Gibbs, I am going to be perfectly frank with you. It is my way, and I consider it the safest way, if not the pleasantest. There is an informant, a spy, if you please, in this store. My actions, words, the talk of customers who come in here and sometimes speak on matters that should be sacred to the Latter-day Saints, at least among themselves, are reported daily to that disgraceful sheet, and dished up to its readers as news, interesting news. Understand, if I am mentioned at all in such a disreputable paper, I prefer to be spoken ill of then praised. But, sir, it is neither pleasant nor bearable to be daily held up to ridicule and scorn those who run and read. Read that, sir."

The irate merchant shook a copy of the morning paper in the face of the young man, in which a certain writer retailed at length scandalous assertions, vulgar insinuations, against the merchant.

Willard read the article with amazement, and at the close of it his cheeks burned with the consciousness that he was the young man alluded to, and his very shame at so unmanly a part being accredited to him, made him look flushed, trembling and unnerved.

"Brother Lang, I don't wonder you are angry. It makes me feel as if I must horsewhip the scoundrel who wrote it."

"It does, eh? How do you feel about the one who was the instigator? Look here, young man, I might as well say it right out. I have suspected you for some time back. You've been mighty intimate with Arthur Willis lately, and week after week, have I read such things in this paper. Don't attempt to deny it, I myself have seen you together many times. Last night I took a quiet walk down to your lodgings, and as I stepped on the porch I heard your voice and that rascal's on the upper one; I didn't listen but concluded not to knock. As I turned away I distinctly heard you say 'Lang's Daughters'; and when this appeared in this lying sheet, I knew only too well where Arthur Willis got his information."

"Hold on a minute, sir, let me ask you a question, who or what is this Arthur Willis that you speak so? Is he not Brother Willis' own nephew?"

"Nephew? Yes, God pity him! But he is, as you ought to know by this time, an apostate and a low-lived blackguard, who lives by slandering and vilifying his father, friends, relatives and anyone, in short, who professes to lead decent lives. He is a frequenter of houses of ill-fame and seeks always to drag young men down to his level, that they may become free American citizens. Why do you ask me what he is, you've known him long enough I should think?"

"Sir, you do me an injustice. I know nothing whatever of his morals or his character."

Yet even as Willard spoke, he remembered half-spoken words, allusions, hints, and even sentences that had struck him as strange, coming from a Mormon youth's mouth, from one whom he had always supposed as pure as a girl – it was for that very reason that he had attributed these chance remarks to ignorance and utterly refused to see any meaning in them. Last night, Arthur had jokingly urged him to pay court to Brother Lang's two young daughters, and thus secure a partnership in the business.

He had replied that he was totally unacquainted with Brother Lang's family, although indeed, he had been invited several times to spend the evening up at the merchant's house. Good heavens! Unsuspicious as a babe, utterly ignorant of what he had been doing, he had acted the part of a betrayer to his employer, a faithful brother in the church.

Rising from his chair in much agitation he faltered, "Brother Lang, I don't wonder you suspect me, but you are all wrong."

Too excited to realize what he was saying, he but added to his guilty appearance.

"It remains to be proven whether I or you are in the wrong. One thing must be done at once. You will have to look for work elsewhere. I cannot employ anyone who could so shamefully abuse the confidence reposed in him. There sir," holding out some money, "is the amount I owe you, and wish you a very good morning."

Stunned, dazed, Willard yet was quick enough to realize he was dismissed in disgrace, and to feel the spirit in which the money was held out to him.

"Keep the money, sir; I will have none of it. You have wronged me bitterly, for I am innocent, although I may have acted and talked foolishly. I was ignorant of the fact which you seem to know so well that Willis is an apostate, I want you to know that. For the present I will say goodbye, Mr. Lang," and he flung himself out of the office, put on his hat and over-coat and shutting up his books with a slam, he at once walked out into the cold of the outer day.

It was a very good thing that Mr. Arthur Willis was not in his room when Willard returned to his lodgings. Good also that he did not return that night. For I very much fear irate Willard would have taken what satisfaction he could get out of that mournful-eyed youth's shrinking frame. Thinking was next to impossible. Going out he purchased the longest, strongest blacksnake he could find in the harness shop, and carried it carefully home.

If he had known where to find Willis, he would have hunted him up; but had heretofore supposed him a clerk in some store.

As the evening wore on, he grew calmer and thought began to take the place of emotion. He went out and paced up and down the upper porch, until the cold air had cooled his head and left him quieter if still full of sadness.

What was he to do? It was winter and he knew it would be very difficult, if indeed at all possible, to get more employment. He had, true to his own nature, spent all that he earned and although not in debt, he was not possessed of ten dollars.

After all, what was the use? The only friend he had made had been a traitor from the first. Why didn't Brother Lang warn him long before?

Talk about this being Zion: Men were, if it were possible, ten times more selfish and exacting, less kind and generous than men in the world. He had not discovered one trace of sociability and altogether Salt Lake City was a town full of rascals and dupes.

These thoughts grew, enlarged, and finally, when he at last returned to his room and sat down by his cheerful little fire, his whole heart was filled with bitterness.

Midnight came and he slowly and mechanically prepared for bed. Turning out his light as mechanically, he turned to the bed and was about to kneel down as he had done every night and morning ever since he had been baptized. Hold on! What was the use of praying? What good had it ever done him? He had given up or had had taken from him everything in life worth having, until now, here he was in a strange city, literally friendless, betrayed, thrown out of work in the dead of winter. Great use his praying had done.

Even as he half spoke the last words aloud, he remembered a sentence in a sermon he had heard President Brigham Young preach: "Whenever I feel so bad that I don't want to pray, I know that then is the very time when I most need praying for."

Was that inspiration or weakness, that remembered sentence? A pause, a struggle, then half-impulsively, almost recklessly, he slipped down on his knees, and repeated over a few words of supplication.

He had conquered the evil for that night at least. His spirit received what he asked for, albeit he had not been as humble as he should have been and always before had been. But God is very good! He dropped off to sleep in a much better frame of mind, saying to himself, "Tomorrow things may look brighter."

Tomorrow and days after came and went, and Willard found his last ten cents gone. I would not be a true chronicler if I did not acknowledge that his soul was tossed to and fro in doubt oftentimes during that miserable time of trial.

One day, it was Thursday, and hearing it was fast day, he had smiled bitterly to himself as he thought, "Not much trouble for you to fast, old boy, you can't do anything else."

He went out upon the street, and seeing the people hastening to the ward houses, he concluded to go to fast meeting. The music and prayer eased the pain in his heart, and in the holy influences of the place and hour he forgot his hunger, his care and trouble.

Toward the close of the meeting a tall, quite elderly sister arose, spoke a few words in tongues. The Bishop told her to use her freedom, all were under the guidance of the Holy Spirit.

She began, and as the strange words issued in a soft, mellow stream of liquid sounds, Willard felt a peculiar bright exaltation of mind creep over him – the same bright, heavenly influence as he had experienced on coming out of the waters of baptism.

She moved down the aisle, still speaking, and waved her arms about as if to include the whole congregation, then as she reached Willard she stopped a moment, and extended her hand and pointing to him she addressed a few words to him.

After she had ceased and resumed her own seat, many were quietly wiping their eyes because of the sweet influence which seemed to fill the whole house.

The Bishop arose and asked if there was anyone in the house who could interpret what the sister had said in tongues, adding that it was necessary for the edification of the Saints for tongues to be interpreted, that all might be blessed in understanding what the Lord had said through the gift.

A sister thereupon arose in another part of the house and poured out in an eloquent flood the interpretation. Blessings and exhortations were given, and she, too, walked down the aisle, stretching out her arms as the former sister had done, prophesying to those who should live to see the appearing of our Savior in a temple built in this land.

Going on down the aisle, she pointed to Willard and said, "Blessed art thou brother, because of thy sacrifices for Christ's sake. God has remembered you, and he will restore you, aye, four-fold. Therefore, be comforted! Lift up your head and rejoice, for you are of the pure in heart. Be not cast down, for all is well. Trials must needs come, and in this think not thou art alone. As gold seven times refined, so shall the Saints be. Therefore press on, the goal is in sight. Be humble and faithful and all will be well with you."

Like a stream of delicious fire her words seemed to pour over his whole soul a divine glory. He felt as if he could face even death, so great was his courage to bear all God might call him to endure. As the sister sat down he found his face bathed in tears, but through and through thrilled a quiet, peaceful influence, causing him to lift his full heart in silent gratitude to God for this manifestation of His mercy.

The Bishop made a few concluding remarks, giving the Saints the key whereby they might always know light from darkness, truth from error.

"Truth," he said, "always brings a spirit of quiet joy, of infinite peace. No noise, no confusion, nothing savoring of rant or riot. All is beautifully calm in the mansions of God, and anything contrary to that spirit comes from the devil, no matter how closely he may imitate the outside appearance of this divine influence. Excitement and noise are from below, quiet and peace from God!"

Willard felt like another man. He walked out of the house filled with love and good fellowship for all mankind. He did not find a trace of bitterness even for the cruel betrayal of himself by Arthur Willis. Instead, a great pity welled up in his heart for the misguided youth, and he felt more like praying for him than cursing him.

As he came out of the house he found the Bishop surrounded by a little group, but as he appeared the good old man stepped aside and said, "Brother Gibbs, I was in Brother Lang's store yesterday and found you had left his employment. Let me take the liberty of asking if you are now at work?"

"No, sir. I wish I was."

"You are a young member of the Church, brother, or you would know that the Bishops are, or try to be, fathers to the people, and when any are in need of assistance or comfort, they should seek us, and we will do all in our power to help them. Are you still lodging at Mrs. —— ?"

"Yes, sir; at least I was there last night, but to be frank with you as you have so kindly asked me, I shall be obliged to leave there at once. I have no money."

"Well, well, and here I knew nothing of all this. The teachers should have known of this."

Willard colored, for he remembered he had purposely absented himself from the evening the teachers usually came around on their monthly visits, being in a somewhat bitter frame of mind.

"I was out, sir, when they called last."

"Oh! Well, now then, brother, come home with me. You can be quite a help to us for a week or two." He added, as he saw the slight hesitation in the young man's manner and guessing its cause, "my own son is going to school and the outside chores fall very heavily on me."

Gladly consenting, he took the proffered arm of his new friend and the two walked slowly toward the Bishop's home, talking over the strange events of the day, Willard gradually opening his heart to the keen, kindly gaze bent on him, and ending with the prophecy uttered by the aged sister that day.

"How strange that she should repeat the very identical words uttered to me when I was so weighed down in my native home, I was to receive four-fold for all I had lost. And then, too, how could she know, except by the Spirit of God, that I was being so bitterly tried and tempted?"

"'God moves in a mysterious way His wonders to perform'," was the hymn sung today. It is even so, Brother Gibbs. But there is one thing I want to tell you that I have seen in this Church. Indeed, I have never known it to fail. When a man or woman embraces the gospel and then emigrates to Zion, they fancy that as soon as they reach here their troubles are all over, when in very truth they have just really begun. The very hardest trials to faith and feeling seem to be given to the Saints immediately on arriving here and for a short time after. I can explain this in the words of President Young. He often says, 'You fancy you have enough of evil influences to contend with in the world; but for every devil,' he is always thus plain in speech, 'you find in the world, you will find a hundred here in Zion; the devil is a good general, and in this hard fight that is going on between him and light eternal he knows enough to mass his strongest and stoutest forces where they are most needed, and that is among the Saints of God.' Hence it is, Brother Gibbs, that we seem to be so tried and beset. But when we do win, we have the greater power and the greater blessings here in Zion. So it is well worth the struggle."

"Yes, I can see that. But why is it that the Saints themselves so try each other?"

"We are all mortal, and as long as we live we will try each other. As Brother Joseph F. says, we will always be rubbing off each other's sharp corners."

They had reached the gate and were now going through the little walk and up to the porch, swept clean of snow, and spotless white were the boards.

Interested in what they were saying, the Bishop stood a moment on the porch to finish the conversation before entering.

"Brother Gibbs, you cannot blame the people for being a little suspicious of you; you are a new member, and it is often the case that the people are deceived by those who enter the fold like wolves in sheep's clothing only to deceive and destroy. Others again, shoot up like a rocket, and quite as often I have discovered descend like one, into darkness and disgrace. Be contented to slowly learn, slowly advance. Learn every lesson well that you may never have to turn back to learn that lesson over again."

Hardly had the last word left his lips before the front door was pulled open violently from the inside, the flying figure of a girl dashed through and perforce fell into Willard's arms.

Quick as a flash, impulsive as always, Willard's arms closed around the panting form and he pressed a quick kiss on the upturned, startled face.

He could have beaten himself for it the next moment. What a fine fool he had acted right on the threshold of his new and sole friend's house; he a stranger. What mad impulse possessed him?

The girl sprang away the moment she was released and ran sobbing back into the house.

Here was a pretty predicament.

Part IV

"Bless my soul!" ejaculated the Bishop.

The young man stood, downcast and ashamed.

His look of evident contrition and shame seemed to bear its own impress of truth to the penetrating eyes of the father, and his frown of displeasure gradually smoothed away.

"Forgive me, sir; and please ask the young lady to pardon so rude and insulting an action. Believe me, it was an impulse of mischief not meanness. It almost seemed like my own frolicsome sister whom I have not seen," he added sadly, "for over a year."

"I could forgive an offense of that sort if I were only sure it would be the last." The old man drew the door to, and said in a low tone, "You were brought up in the world, Brother Gibbs, and I do not of course know what your manners are. But I warn you to be very circumspect and careful with my girls. They are as innocent as young kittens. And they are as precious to me as the apple of my eye. But there, Brother, I feel that I can trust you, and that you will not disabuse my confidence."

"Thank you, sir," earnestly and simply answered the youth.

Together they entered the house, and a calling to a lady in an inner room the Bishop said,

"Mother, here is Brother Gibbs. You have seen him I guess in meeting. I have asked him to stay with us a few weeks and help me about the work."

Willard sees a lady of medium height, rather stout, about forty-five, with dark blue eyes and dark brown hair that is silvering over with time and care; the face full of a serene, sweet beauty, the straight Grecian nose, tender sensitive mouth, broad, low brow, and through the eyes a shining loveliness of spirit that appealed at once to all the best of his nature.

He shook her outstretched hand and bowed over it with real homage.

"You are welcome, Brother Gibbs, sit down and make yourself at home." The kindly words were uttered in a sweet though rather loud voice, and the manner was as gentle, gracious and winning as that of a duchess.

"Can that be the mother of the little flyaway I was so rude to?" was the thought that crossed his mind.

"Where's Aunt Fannie?"

"She is just getting on the dinner."

"Well, call the folks, and we'll have dinner."

Just then Willard spied a youth of about fourteen who seemed ready to break into an irrepressible laugh. He sobered down though as soon as he found he was being observed.

"Tommy, this is Brother Gibbs; come and shake hands, my son."

The irrepressible youth walked quickly up to Willard and said without the least trace of embarrassment, "How do ye do, Brother Gibbs."

Willard felt compelled to answer this western salutation in the answering phrase, "Pretty well, thank you, how are you?"

"Oh, I'm first class," responded Master Tom.

The Bishop led the way through the hall into a back room where a number of people stood apparently waiting for their coming.

"This is my wife Fanny, and my wife Sarah. Moroni, my eldest son, and Lovina, my eldest daughter. Where is Rhoda, mother?"

"She is busy upstairs, Father."

Willard instantly surmised that the absent Rhoda was the one he had met so unceremoniously.

Quite a number of children of both sexes and all ages crowded around the table and took apparently their usual places.

"Where shall we have Brother Gibbs sit, Fanny?"

"Right between you and Moroni, Father," and all were at last seated.

Willard saw there were no vacant seats and guessed that Miss Rhoda would not appear at this meal.

"What a stupid ass I have made myself appear," was his inward comment; for his conduct had so abashed him that he appeared awkward, ill at ease, and reserved.

He felt too nervous to notice any of the assembled family very closely, but observed that the young girl her father called "Lovina" sat at the foot of the table, as far away from himself as possible.

The glimpses he had of her face made him sure that she was the daughter of the first wife he had been introduced to; he scarcely knew why, but nevertheless he felt it was so.

That evening, the Bishop took him out to the stables and corrals and together they did the evening chores. Tommy was allowed to accompany his brother Moroni to the evening classes of the school which the elder brother attended so faithfully.

"You see," explained the father, "I have had to work hard all my life; and as soon as Moroni was old enough, I had to have his help. So he hasn't had much schooling. And now in the winter I give him all the chances I can. I am glad, too, that Thomas can get to go a little, for he has lots o' work to do and don't get any more schooling than his brother."

Willard looked at the huge barn piled high with hay, the granaries rich with grain, the stock, the fowls, the horses and hogs, and knowing that this man dug his families' daily food out of mother earth with his two hands, assisted in summers by his boys, he did not wonder that the boys had not had "much schooling."

It took them both over an hour to complete the "chores," and it was quite dark when they came back into the house, stamping the snow from their shoes as they came in.

"You're a bad, wicked boy, and I almost hate you," they heard uttered in a loud, shrill tone of anger as the Bishop opened the door.

"Rhoda, Thomas, what do you mean?" expostulated another voice.

"See here," as the flying form of his daughter dashed out into the hall and from the patter of feet upstairs into the upper regions; the Bishop stood still. "Mother, what's all this about?"

Tommy stood up behind a chair evidently equally divided between fear of his father's displeasure and a loud, boisterous laugh.

"Oh," answered mother, "it's Tommy plaguing Rhoda again. I do wish they would not be so quarrelsome."

"What do you mean, Thomas? Aren't you ashamed to tease the girls?" somewhat austerely demanded the father.

"No, Sir, not very," frankly answered the boy, a grin almost gaining the ascendancy.

"Well, then you'd ought to. If it's about that wishbone, I want it understood once and for all that I forbid you or any other member of my family speaking of it again, anywhere or any place. Do you understand, Thomas? You carry your frolics too far sometimes."

"Yes, sir," responded the now subdued Tommy.

Shortly after, the Bishop took down from the old-fashioned mantle shelf a large bell, and going to the door he rang it with great deliberation and with exact precision.

Into the long dining room trooped the whole family. A little chat, questions and answers from the elders to each other, and then the good man said, "Come, let us have prayers."

This was Willard's first insight into a polygamous family, and he was quick to note every feature of the family life.

After the comprehensive but rather long prayer in which the young man faithfully followed every word, the brief rustle subsided, and he began to more closely observe the various members of this, to him, singular family.

The girl whom he had heard called Lovina sat next to the wife the Bishop usually addressed as "mother." He had time in the general conversation that followed to notice the perfect loveliness of her face and head. Pure pearly skin, eyes of blue, small sweet mouth, high rounded brow "like her father's," his mental comment – arching neck, delicate features, even the ears being so small and perfect they were like two ocean shells, the light-brown hair being parted and combed back, and braided down on the shoulders. Her dress was dark, but pale blue ribbons set off the lovely complexion, and when he had completed his brief examination, he involuntarily exclaimed to himself as many had done before him, "how beautiful." The expression of the face was somewhat cold and reserved, but the tender lines about the mouth, "it is her mother's mouth," was his thought, betrayed a nature full of affection and capable, perhaps, of passionate tenderness.

But, where is Rhoda? Was his mental query as he glanced about the group and saw no one of the half grown lassies here or there that seemed to be the one he had held for one moment in his arms.

The Bishop's mind seemed full of the same thought and he said aloud, "Where is my daughter Rhoda?"

"She is upstairs, Father," answered mother, who Willard guessed was really Rhoda's mother.

"Well," said the father, "tell her after this I want her to come to her meals and to prayers. You can tell her that Brother Gibbs is as sorry and ashamed of his part of that silly affair as she seems to be. He has asked mine and her forgiveness and I am willing, for this once," slowly emphasizing, "to overlook it. He will behave himself in the future, of that I am sure. I only wish I were equally sure that Rhoda would act a little less like a great tom-boy."

"Oh, Pa," exclaimed Lovina from her corner, "Rhoda is nothing but a child."

"Well, well, that's enough on that subject. Now then, go and call her down, and we'll have a little music before we go to bed."

The boys, Moroni and Tom, came in at that moment from night school, and in the general moving and bustle, Willard failed to note the little figure that slipped in the door and dropped down on the melodian stool. Not until a few chords from the organ were struck did the slight confusion subside and he caught sight of the organist.

Yes, that was Rhoda. He recognized with a thrill the lithe, round figure, every curve and line being a perfect symmetry. She had the same light-brown hair as her sister Lovina, he could see that. But a something in the sauce poise of the head showed him she was not like the quiet, reserved, elder sister.

The voice rose and fell in the quaint, old song of "When You and I Were Young, Maggie." Most the family joined in the chorus, the little ones even dragging two bars behind or jumping gaily along a bar ahead of the rest.

A few sprightly tunes, "dancing tunes," Aunt Fanny explained to him, followed the song which she told him was "father's favorite."

The Bishop spoke to Moroni during a pause in the music, and then perforce the organist ceased, and swinging round on her stool, she quietly slipped away into the darkest corner; but it was not yet so dark that Willard could not at odd times observe her thus, noting the downcast face.

She was not as beautiful as Lovina, but she was still very pretty. As the good-nights were exchanged, he saw that Lovina was taller, more slender, but had a graceful rounded form; not as plump as Rhoda's, but in truth they were both, he decided, lovely girls in face and form.

The Bishop lingered with Willard to tell him somewhat concerning his duties, and then taking a candle he led the way upstairs to the "boy's room," and showed him a single bed across from the one where the two oldest boys slept and with a hearty good-night, left the young man to his own thoughts.

The two lads were asleep, and he quickly undressed, blew out his light and bowed down in humble fervent prayer. As he prayed he thought of the day's proceedings, the manifestations of God's mercy to him, and then – his ungentlemanly, rude conduct on the threshold of his new home. He asked to be pardoned and that the circumstance might be forgiven and completely forgotten by his kind friends, adding an earnest promise which he felt was a covenant to God that, while he dwelt under that roof, he would in word and deed respect the wishes of his host and would never again offer the least familiarity to any daughter of the house.

As he lay thinking it all over afterward, he could hardly explain it to himself. Not in any way a woman-hater, quite the contrary, he had still felt too much reverence and respect to all his girl friends, even in boyhood, to offer the least freedom that might offend the delicate sensibilities of girlhood.

It was an impulse, he could only decide, born of his love for romping and mischief, and should be most carefully guarded against in the future. What had come over him? Was he beginning to forget his wife, his own wife, although separated from her? No, a thousand times no! She was his own, and no other would or should come between his heart and her image. He should be true to her, no matter what the cost.

With this firm resolve his mind drifted from Hortense to the boy he had never seen, and as he had done ever since he left home, he fell asleep praying for their peace and comfort.

Part V

The days swept into weeks, and spring at last broke up the snowy bands that winter had clasped around the earth, and the great brown face of our faithful Mother began to show through the melting snows of March.

Willard had become pretty well acquainted with his friends, the Mainwarings – the cheerful, honest, intelligent father, with a nature as strong as iron but made beautiful by the soft velvet folds of love and charity engendered by a faithful observance of the gospel laws – him Willard loved even as a father. The man was indeed one to be loved. Devoted to his religion, he sought to make his daily life comport with his constant teachings. Stern in rebuke, he yet healed the wound his sharpness had made with the oil of a greater kindness, a more tender thoughtfulness. When these rebukes had been administered, sometimes, a few times even to him, the after tenderness of his manner often recalled to Willard's mind the passage in the Doctrine and Covenants:

"Reproving betimes with sharpness, when moved upon by the Holy Ghost, and then showing forth afterwards an increase of love towards him whom thou hast reproved, lest he esteem thee to be his enemy."

There was a lofty dignity of character about Bishop Mainwaring that commanded men's homage, while his overflowing love and kindness won their confidence and affection.

He had also become acquainted with the lovely character of the first wife Mary, "mother" as she was so frequently called by the members of the family, her generous forgetfulness of self and her pure, earnest faith. Fanny, the second wife, was likewise a good, true woman, with a quick, lively disposition, accompanied by a somewhat sharp tongue; yet she was withal so quick to forget and forgive, so ready to help with the hands while she scolded with the lips that he was willing to grasp the prickly outside so quickly that it didn't hurt and find gladly the kernel of goodness and truth beneath the sharp exterior.

Sarah, the third wife, puzzled him. At first he had fancied she was the kinder, the sweetest dispositioned of the three. Her words were so soft and so gentle, uttered in a low, quick monotone with a deprecatory manner that at the first acquaintance made one feel that she was the genuine philanthropist, if not a real martyr.

This first experience of his in a polygamous family made a deep impression upon him, and he found himself studying intently the daily drama of life spread out before his eyes.

He could not fail to see that "Aunt Fanny's" (as he grew to call her) acerbity of tongue was directed most frequently at "Aunt Sarah's" seemingly defenseless head. Even he heard little sharp slings thrown at Aunt Sarah, who always retreated in oceans of tears and – it must be confessed – with a telling retort clothed in Aunt Sarah's own soft, low tones and martyrized manner.

Never in his life had he become so intimately acquainted with the female character, and never before had he realized the heights to which woman steps in her grand unselfishness, the depths to which her petty intrigues and self-absorbed desires cast her down.

It was late in the spring, and he was busy, as were all hands, putting in spring crops and doing general spring work.

Moroni was a good, faithful boy, much like his father, and soon won a warm place in Willard's affectionate nature.

But Tommy, bright, active, honest, careless, heedless Tommy, witty, and as full of mischief as a young monkey, Tommy claimed Willard's deepest love and tenderness. He was Aunt Fanny's only child, delicate in frame and growing so fast, "spindling up" his father called it, that he crept into the lonely heart of the young man like a dear younger brother. He could never feel angry with the rogue, and often longed to second him in his frolics, but would not – his first blunder never left his mind.

Tommy often boyishly betrayed family secrets to him, and when they did not savor too much of the "inner sanctuary" he always allowed the boy to chatter.

"We are going to the farm today, Will. Are you going along?"

"I don't know," answered Willard.

"Well, I hope you are. You know father's going down to set the men to work on the new house."

"Are you going to have a new house down there for all hands?"

"Oh, no," approaching him and whispering, "the family are going to meet in solemn conclave and appoint Aunt Sarah as a missionary to the farm," and the eyes danced.

"Why, Thomas, was a sacrilegious boy you are."

"Am I? Well, you live in our house a few years, and if you don't want to move out on the farm or else petition Aunt Sarah to, I am mistaken."

"I don't understand what you mean by speaking of your Aunt Sarah so. I never saw a better woman in my life."

"Oh, she's good enough. Awful good. So good it takes an angel from heaven to live with her."

"You shock me, Tommy. I am ashamed of you."

"Well, don't be. I like Aunt Sarah. Real well, too. Only it's like I like real sweet blackberries. Soon cloy on 'em, and only want to see 'em a few times a year."

Tommy discreetly left Willard to digest his similes at his leisure and walked into the stable and began to hitch up the double-seated "light wagon."

When they were ready to drive out, the Bishop came out and asked Willard if he would like to go down with them, which offer was gladly accepted.

There was a bustle of excitement as the little crowd came out of the gate and settled into their respective places. Children crowded at the door to say "good-bye, mamma," and to see them off.

"Where am I going?" nervously asked Aunt Sarah with a slight laugh. "You will, of course, prefer someone else in with you, won't you, father, for I am such a coward. You know what a coward I always was, father, and Tommy is such a poor driver," and she fluttered and fussed.

"You can sit behind in the carriage, Sarah," said the Bishop. "Willard was going along to help Thomas if he needs any help, and this colt here is so frisky that I feel somewhat nervous myself to drive him. So, Fanny, as you are the bravest one in the Mainwaring family, you can risk yourself along o' me."

"Oh," murmured Aunt Sarah as she began to climb into the carriage, "I thought pa said for me to come with him. He knows I'd sooner risk myself behind wild horses if he held the lines than with cows driven by a baby."

The soft, murmuring, deprecatory manner and tone appealed to Willard, who was all sympathy at once for poor Aunt Sarah. But something in the words themselves seemed to sting Tommy, for he gave the steady old farm horse a cut that sent them plunging ahead, almost into the buggy.

"Oh-h," shrieked Aunt Sarah.

"Tommy," scolded Rhoda, who was just about to sit down, the jerk sending her almost into Willard's lap.

"Oh, dear," wailed Aunt Sarah softly as she pressed her baby in her arms, "I just know we'll all be dashed out and killed. I feel sure of it. Stop the carriage, Tommy and I'll walk back."

Neither Tommy nor anyone else believed she meant a word of the last sentence, so he plunged on, fire in his eyes, his youthful mouth set. He was silent for a wonder, which fact made both Rhoda and Aunt Mary feel that every rock in the road would receive full attention from him. The colt flew over the long, straight road to the south where the farm lay, and Tommy recklessly dashed after him. Every "sidling" place was carefully selected and when reached the horses were urged almost into a gallop.

"We shall all be killed," moaned Aunt Sarah again and again.

"Don't think about it," said wise mother, "just put your mind on something else. You will get yourself all worked up into a perfect fever. Come, let's talk of something else. Willard, do you know when the new house is to be begun?"

"No, ma'am. I have not heard the Bishop mention the matter."

"I heard father say," said Rhoda, "that it would be ready to go into by August. Say, mother, do you know who's going to live down there? Won't it be lovely for the one who does?"

"No, I don't know, dear. I supposed father will let us women folks arrange that to suit ourselves."

"Well, I know of one," said Aunt Sarah, "who will not be allowed to go in there. I have never owned a thing in my life, not even a tin cup. Always have had to ask for the use of every single thing. I don't suppose that while I live on this earth I shall ever be permitted to call a cup mine, let alone a house and home. Why is it that some seem to have all the blessings and others all the crosses? My comfort is that it won't be so in heaven. We shall get our righteous dues there, and be understood as we are. Oh-h, Tommy Mainwaring, are you going to kill us all and send us unprepared into eternity?"

"I thought, Aunt Sarah, you were longing to go."

"What a wicked, perverse boy you are. How could you imagine such a thing?"

"I am sure," quietly observed Aunt Mary at this juncture, "we all fare alike in father's household. He deals justly by us all. If one has any advantage in one way, pa is sure to make it up to the others in another way."

I am taking you behind the scenes in this family, even as Willard found himself, for he was soon looked upon by the simple, guileless folk as one of themselves.

If you think poor Tom was disrespectful or Aunt Sarah odd, you must bear in mind that plural marriage is of most benefit in that very thing, that it trains us – if we will let it – to become more charitable, more loving and unselfish to all.

Willard listened rather vaguely to all the talk, for his thoughts were nearer home. Indeed, thought was merged into emotion, and he had besides much ado to preserve his equilibrium during the repeated jolts and jumps caused by Tom's reckless driving.

Occasionally, when a very "tippy place," as Rhoda called it, came along, he would see Tom's eyes flash into Rhoda's as he mischievously whipped up the horses to greater speed, while Rhoda's eyes danced with fun.

The bracing air sweet with all the rejuvenating influences of the young spring, the grassy lanes lined with dandelions' gay banners and the faint loveliness of the flowers, the scene of rural beauty, fields of rich brown loam just turned over for planting, streams of water here and there like measured lines of silver, the tall trees lining the roadside and casting their light shadows of young green athwart the path, the green meadows, and over and around all, the great towering peaks of old Wasatch; all this entered the consciousness of the young man's artistic temperament, and he leaned out to gaze with quiet rapture on the scene. He said something of this to his companion, and Rhoda answered, "I love the mountains. They are the retreat and the defense of my parents and their people. But I long to see the world. The great big world. What is the world like? Are there mountains and valleys, and are people out there just like our people? I have seen outsiders, you know, but some way they seem different, more polite, more refined than we are. Now, you are almost an outsider, you know."

The gay laugh, the implied compliment so innocently given, caused Willard to look down quickly into the suddenly raised grey eyes beside him. Then they both laughed; she in confusion, he in merriment.

The last corner was turned, the clump of trees with the old log house where they always camped was at hand, and Tom drove up with a dash and clatter, his eyes twinkling with mischief, and so riotous a plunge did the poor goaded horses give that even Aunt Fanny called out sharply, "Thomas, do you see what you are about?"

The Bishop stepped out from the trees where he had just tied his colt, Willard jumped down and hasted round to assist Aunts Sarah and Mary to alight, while Rhoda hopped off the wheel like a bird.

"He will not even offer me his hand to help me out of a wagon," she thought sadly.

"Well, father," murmured Sarah, "we have had a narrow escape. And it's been nothing on earth but my faith that has kept us from being dashed into eternity."

Thereupon Tom burst into a loud, irrepressible laugh, merrily joined by Rhoda, and even Willard smiled and smiled until the contagion spread, and he too laughed aloud.

"Say, sis, just look in the bottom of the carriage for that mustard seed, will you?"

Another ripple of merriment, and Aunt Sarah inquired plaintively why it was that the children were ever finding so much to laugh about. For her, she could almost cry with relief to be out of that engine of death, the carriage. She hoped never to go through such another scene of torture, no, not for an hour. She was all this while searching for the mustard seed which Tom had said pa brought down for planting.

"I can't find that seed," she said at last, "have you lost it, Tommy?"

"No, ma'am," the boy answered. "I think it must have been spilled by the wayside."

"What seed?" interposed the Bishop. "I haven't brought any seed. Come on now, all hands, and let us decide where and how to build."

After much talk and many suggestions, a little knoll not far from the spring and its encircling grove of cottonwood trees was decided upon as the most desirable spot.

"Where Fanny or Mary could build their milk house," murmured Aunt Sarah in quite audible tones as she stood between her husband and Willard. "What a comfort it would be to Fanny to know she could be all to herself and could do just as she pleased, with no one to say why do ye so, and the lovely bracing air and pretty scene and all, it is enough to make some poor unfortunate women almost sick with resolving not to break the tenth commandment. I never look for such happiness as this, not I; when all else are served and happy and comfortable, then perhaps, if I am not in my grave long before, then maybe it will come my turn. But it's all right. I never feel to murmur at the dealings of Providence, no matter what I am called on to undergo."

While this rapid monologue was rolling off his wife's smooth tongue, the Bishop stood silent, occasionally turning a keen look into the speaker's face as if to read her real meaning.

Everybody was busy pointing out this or that, and a subdued hum of talk buzzed through the little group.

"Well, now then," said the Bishop in a loud tone, whereat everybody stopped to listen, "It is my intention to build a home for every one of my wives just as soon as means afford. But as this seems to be a necessary move to make down here, now I shall put this one up first. I want the woman who is going to live here to say what kind of a house she wants and to help me to plan it out. So, the very first thing to be done is to find out who's going to live here. Now don't all speak at once, yet all must speak out their minds that we may move understandingly and do things as we'd ought to, by common consent."

Almost before the last word was out of his mouth Aunt Sarah cooed softly,

"Well, I have no call to speak at all, for I hope I know when to speak and when not. So of course I shall stand by and patiently wait till my turn. What is it the Bible says about the first being last in eternity and the last first?" She turned inquiringly with her little joke to Willard, laughing in her subdued way.

"Mother," said the Bishop, "now you are the oldest woman and naturally the first choice rests with you. What do you say?"

"Well, father, I would like to go and I would hate to go. I feel to leave the matter in your hands. You choose for us."

"Some folks know how to choose for themselves," murmured Aunt Sarah.

"Fanny, seeing mother hasn't any choice in the matter, you can tell us your mind."

"Well, I'm sure I don't know what to say. My health ain't very good or else I would jump at the chance. Even as it is, I think I might manage with my boy's help." The subdued murmur of Aunt Sarah's tones reached her ear, and in a quick, impulsive way she said, "Let Sarah come if she wants to so bad. I am quite contented at the old home."

"I am sure," faintly replied Sarah, "I have never given out the least idea that I am bad off to come. How anyone could accuse me of such a thing –"

"Sarah," said the Bishop, "would you like to have this for your permanent home?"

"What a question to pounce on one so suddenlike; let Fanny have her say out first and then I am sure I can –"

"My girl," said the Bishop in an unmistakably clear tone, "answer me right out, do you feel to choose this for your permanent home to be deeded to you and your children?"

"Well, yes, pa, I suppose I shall be willing to go where I'm sent and stay where I'm put. I've never been anything but an obedient, faithful wife, always willing to offer my all on the altar of sacrifice; and if you require this now at my hands, why then, pa, let me say that you will find me ready and willing, no matter what it may –"

The Bishop had turned away, but the last few sentences brought him back, and he said firmly, "Sarah, I do not require sacrifices at the hands of my wives save those what all wives freely give the man they marry and which in turn I am more than willing to return in kind. If you think I am asking you to come here, you are mistaken. Fanny –"

"Oh, pa," she interrupted hurriedly, "I have told you I am more than willing to come. Shall I go down on my knees to say it?" and a great gush of quick tears, that afterwards disappeared as suddenly as they came, poured down her cheeks.

The plans were then discussed, and Aunt Sarah almost forgot her troubles in the excitement of arranging for doors and windows, rooms and closets.

The long shadows cast by the trees gave warning that time pressed, or the men would be late with their chores.

As soon as the start was made for the buggies, Aunt Sarah turned faint and declared herself utterly unable to return in that carriage.

"The strain and job has made my back so I can't endure another thing. I was up nearly all night long last night –"

"Willard," called the Bishop, "do you feel like driving the colt back? If you do, I'll get into the carriage and take these cowardly girls of mine in with me."

"I shall be quite willing, sir."

"Then let's see, who shall go with you?"

"Father, I should prefer going back in the carriage," announced frank Aunt Fanny.

"Of course you will. Well, I don't see any other way but for you to take Rhoda and Tom, too. There'll be room for all. And with careful driving you'll get home safe."

This seemed more pleasant all around, and the whole party started home in gay spirits.

That long-to-be-remembered ride! How the fiery young horse bent his head and, disdaining the restraining pressure in his mouth, flew over the road like the unloosed wind. Willard set his teeth and held onto the slender reins, devoutly praying that they would not break under the strain, for they were old and worn. The cool breeze became in their rapid flight a stinging wind. Trees along the road dashed past like "fence poles," as Tom afterwards said. The soft, springy loam flew off the colt's feet in great clumps back in the buggy, and sometimes in their laps.

Even Tommy's face grew white as they neared the city, and he realized the danger of the many turnings and the deep creeks to be crossed ere they reached their own home.

Not a word for miles.

Then Willard half-whispered to the silent little figure at his side, "Are you afraid?"

"No," she answered, and added under her breath, "not with you."

He was scarcely sure of what she said, but her low, intense tone of confidence and trust thrilled him to his very finger tips.

"I am glad," he answered softly.

The buggy swayed to and fro as crossing after crossing was passed, and at last here is home.

Thank heaven, someone has undone the gate, and the colt dashes in, grazing the wheel on the gate post, Moroni jumps at his bits and the creature stands trembling in every limb, while Willard quickly jumps out and unharnesses him.

"Why," calls Lovina, "you three look as if you had seen a ghost."

"I think I have," assents Willard, as the face of his wife gazes reproachfully into his heart.

"Willard, my boy," he says to himself, "you and I must have a reckoning."

"Come in folks," urges Lovina, "we've had company all the afternoon."

"Who, Lov?" asks Tom.

"Come in and see," and then as Willard follows her she says, "Brother Gibbs, allow me to make you acquainted with Sister Lang and Miss Phoebe Lang and Miss Aseneth Lang."

Coloring to the very roots of his dark hair, Willard goes forward to shake hands with the mother and her two tall, lady-like daughters. For the malicious taunts of a vile newspaper, in relation to himself and these girls, make him so ashamed, as he remembers them, that even gentle Mrs. Lang wonders if he really was the instigator of the rumors.

The Bishop opportunely enters, and, greeting Sister Lang in his hearty yet dignified way, the talk is general, and Willard goes out to do the evening chores.

When he comes back he finds Sister Lang and the Bishop absent from the little group gathered about the center table.

"Say, Will," says Tommy, "we're trying to coax Phoebe and 'Seneth to spend the evening."

"If they will," adds Rhoda, "we'll go over and get some of the Gibson boys and girls, and ma says we can make some molasses candy and have some games."

"Will, you and I can get Mame and Hattie, can't we?" queries Moroni. Only that everything Moroni says is uttered in so quiet and even a voice, one might almost fancy there was a spice of mischief in his remarks.

"If it is so decided, I am quite willing," replies Willard.

It is decided, and away hurry the young men, while the girls make up more fire and bring in the molasses jug, preparatory for the evening's fun.

"Don't have any kissing games, girls," remarks Lovina; "I don't like them one bit."

"You don't!" exclaims Aseneth as she flies around, helping to get everything ready. "Why, I think they are fun."

"Lov, don't," asserts Rhoda; "she would rather be whipped than be kissed by a man. Now, you know, I don't think anything about it."

"Neither do I," says jolly Aseneth. "I just turn my cheek and shut my eyes, and it's over in a second."

"I do hope Sam Gibson won't come, 'cause I just won't join in the kissing games if he is here, that's all there is about it. I can't bear him to kiss me," remarks Lovina.

"Nor I," chorused the other three.

"My own brothers, nor even Willard."

"Oh-h!" says Rhoda.

"Now, don't fly off at a tangent, sis; I am not in love with Willard, if he is handsome. I leave that for such scatter brains as yourself."

"You needn't talk like that, Lou. I am not in love with him either."

Aseneth looked at both girls, and drew her own conclusions.

"Well, here we all are!" called the boys from the hall, as they stamped off the snow and hung up hats and overcoats.

The general dining room was also sitting room and work room. The house was built as so many New England homes were built years ago; a style which is the least beautiful on the outside and the most comfortable on the inside of any style I know. A hall in front, with large, square rooms on each side, chambers above, and at the back a long dining room with kitchen and pantry. A board kitchen at the side of the back door serves as store room in the winter and stove room in the summer. Just now the large room is carpeted with a bright, clean rag carpet, a long table runs up and down the room, wooden chairs are ranged against the wall, the large cookstove makes a cozy warmth from its bright surface, while two large lamps at either end of the table make light enough for all in the room to work and to study.

Harry Wilson and Burt Harmon came in with Moroni so that the long room was full of merry voices and bright young faces.

"It will be an hour before the candy will be ready," Moroni said. "Let's enjoy ourselves meanwhile. What games shall we play?"

A noisy selection of favorite games follows, and, all having decided, a gay scramble – which is called the "Family coach" – sets everybody jumping, and bobbing, and whirling, and running. "Simon says, 'Thumbs up!'" bring out a few forfeits. Then "Spat out and spat in," a genuine upright and downright kissing game, and Willard absorbs the spirit of the evening and forgets everything but the merry mischief of the hour.

The last game, with numerous forfeits to redeem, came all too soon for the two young hearts. A post office was instituted, and when it came Willard's turn, he told Tommy, who was postmaster, that he had a letter for Miss Rhoda with two stamps on it. His heart beat almost to suffocation, as he stood waiting, while Tommy bawled out that "Willard has a letter with twenty-two stamps on it for Rho – da!" drawing out her name.

"I don't believe it, Tommy Mainwaring," cried poor Rhoda; 'you are teasing me."

"Say, Will," opening the door, "did you or did you not say you had a letter for my unworthy sister Rhoda?"

"Yes," answered Willard.

"How many stamps?" asked Moroni, who guessed the trouble.

"Two," said unabashed and wondering Willard in a breath.

"I knew," answered Rhoda, trying to walk with indifference and dignity across the room. As she passed into the hall, Tommy shut the door between the couple and the crowded room.

"Candy's cooked!" called out Aseneth.

This was the signal for the general confusion, and everyone was soon busily engaged in greasing plates and washing hands, preparatory to the "pulling."

As the door shut behind Rhoda, she and Willard stood in the dimly lighted hall, looking into each other's eyes. At last he whispered, "Will you forgive me?" and, as he spoke, he opened his arms impulsively.

Rhoda was so close to him, she could almost hear his heart beat. She hesitated – then, with a quick motion, she put one hand on his shoulder and felt herself drawn close to the breast of the man she loved with all her true, fond young heart.

"May I kiss you?" – and twice he pressed his lips against her own, murmuring, "My little love!"

Instantly the door flew open, and Tommy squealed, "End of scene first!"

Rhoda sprang into the room and, with great clatter and dash, joined in the candy pulling. Willard followed more leisurely, and bore the good-natured taunts of the few witnesses to the little scene with good-natured calmness. Few had profited by Tommy's wicked exposure, and only Aunt Sarah, who sat close by the door, chided Tommy, telling him, jokingly:

"Little boys should not be too smart, for sometimes they get themselves into trouble as well as other folks. Not," she added in an aside to Sister Lang, who sat near her, "that I admire young people carrying on in that way, either. But, of course, Brother Gibbs is from the world, and no one expects him to be as well behaved as our home raised boys are. As for Rhoda – well, you know some folks imagine girls can take their lives and conduct in their hands and go unscathed through a sea of fire. Such freedom – I've often said it comes to no good; why, Sister Lang, my girls – when they grow up – they would never, no never, pretend to such behavior –"

On and on rambled Aunt Sarah's voice, no break, no pause, unless a stray remark from her listener compelled a short rest.

The candy was pulled, boys and girls joined in a game of romp and fun. Some were rough – too rough, being saucy if not rude, while more than one sticky mass lodged in whiskers and hair. Rhoda and Tommy had drawn apart from the rest and were busily engaged in "pulling" a plateful to a high degree of whiteness, which was to be braided in strands and presented, finally, to their father and mothers, who were upstairs.

Suddenly Sam Gibson discovered them and their plateful of daintily arranged candy, and darted into their corner to have a "grab."

Rhoda sprang away, plate in hand, and then followed a race, and two or three joined in the supposed fun. Out of the room at last flew Rhoda, followed closely by Sam, Moroni, and Harry.

"Boys, you hold her," said Sam, who was close upon her, "and I'll take the plate."

As Harry sprang to catch her, he was pushed aside by Willard, who could not bear that anyone should touch her but himself, and seeing the boys were determined to take the candy, whether or no, he firmly locked his arms around the struggling girl and held her, despite the angry – "How dare you, sir," which she flung at him from between her shut teeth. As the last prettily braided stick disappeared from the plate, the poor child surrounded by great, strong, mischievous boys, held in durance vile by the one she thought, above all, she be her protector and help. She cried out shrilly, "You are a mean, cowardly set, and I hate you all," and up flew the tiny slipper from her foot, as she gave a vicious kick to emphasize her remarks.

"Oh-oh!" screeched Tommy.

Away darted Rhoda. Just as her father appeared at the head of the stairs, with the slipper in his hand. It had lit on the landing above as he opened his door to ascertain the cause of the unusual noise.

Tommy entered volubly into the required explanations, shielding Rhoda from blame as bravely as he could. Dwelling pitifully on the labor they had faithfully performed for "dear father" destroyed by the vandals who stood in open mouthed wonder at Tommy's swift denunciations.

A twinkle in the eyes and a sigh in the voice of the good old Bishop betrayed the mingled sorrow and sympathy of the father.

"I will have a talk with Rhoda or her mother tomorrow," decided the Bishop, in his own mind, as he slowly ascended the stairway.

The young men went back into the dining room, rather ashamed of the part they had taken in the affair.

Sorry, doubly sorry, for his part, Willard turned into the dining room and resolved to seize the first chance to explain matters to Rhoda.

He had no chance that evening, for she was not again visible below stairs.

As the visitors began to depart, about eleven o'clock, Willard saw that the young men had all "gone home" with one or the other, leaving Mrs. Lang and her two daughter without an escort.

Common politeness urged him to offer his services, and together they set out for the home of his former employer.

Refusing the kind invitation to go in and sit a moment, the young man hastened home in the vain hope that Rhoda might be downstairs, assisting in the general cleaning up of the untidy scene of the night's frolic.

Entering the dining room, he felt a keen pang of disappointment to find the room empty save for Aunt Sarah, who was busy putting the finishing touches to the straightening process.

"Folks all went off to bed," she said in answer to his look of unconscious inquiry. "Seems like I can't go to bed and leave things in an uproar. None but those who have to do it know how hard it is to be the one to keep things going; drop an end and ravel goes a whole yard. I'm tire plum to death; but there, you know, I have to growl so much. I'm ashamed of growling; I often say that Tommy and I do the grunting for the whole family."

"I am sorry we have made you so much work tonight, Aunt Sarah. Let me help you if I can."

"Oh, you can't do anything. Men, you know, are so awkward. Just lift that table back – there, that's it; and there, set this chair in the corner.

That's what the Bishop says, 'boys are a useless lot in the house;' I tell him sometimes boys have to live anyhow."

"Did Rhoda feel angry at us?" He could resist the temptation no longer to find out how far he had offended.

"Rhoda is an odd girl. Good, you know; but that's just what I said to her, when she said men raised in the world was not what they ought to be, that we ought to have more charity for them then. Good gracious! If we were all weighed in the balance, we'd be found wanting a good deal."

"She thought I was the chief offender, then, did she?"

"Well, you know, when a man has run away from a wife – not but what, as I told her, a man must leave father and mother, wife and children, for his religion; but, you know, girls don't stop to think of that part of it. As I told her, even if it did kill her respect for a man, she shouldn't be so free to express it. Besides, what was such a trifling thing as the candy fracas of tonight, a cause for the silly child saying it showed her the cruel nature of such a man, so that she should hate him forever. I told her if a woman like a man, abuse and injustice didn't kill it all at once. But, la! She just declared, then, she'd kill it or kill herself. She is such a girl to talk. As for me, I can't see no sense in always talking, talking, talking. Why can't we live like Saints do? If we ain't Saints, we ought to be; and we'd ought to live in peace and harmony every day of our lives. That's what I say to the Bishop, not much use in going to meetings and be always professing like we must just live like Saints at home. Going up to bed? Well, I don't wonder you are tired – especially of such frivolous hoydens as some of our girls are. But there, girls act different to what my mother allowed her girls –"

Poor Willard was obliged to leave the room while the monologue was in full force. But Aunt Sarah was also ready to leave, and on up the stairs the gentle, pattering words rippled relentlessly on; even at his door she stood still, offering and answering remarks, with good natured tolerance of his silence, as oblivious of the drawn, white face which was only partly turned to her as she was of his evident anxiety to escape. With a last effort, he turned the door knob, and, as the door opened, Tommy's unmistakable snore set Aunt Sarah's tongue off on a fresh subject, which followed Willard even after he had retreated to the sheltering darkness of the chamber.

Once really alone, he cast himself prone on his bed and through him raced and sped the very angels of agony and despair. He could not think, could not reason, was not even aware of the whole cause of this horrible distress. His hands clenched in his hair, the painful sensation consequent thereon relieving, in some measure, the pain in his mind. He lay for hours, his soul dully rebellious, his body occasionally shaken with dry, harsh sobs. Like phantom nightmares, visions of his wife, whom he had loved and still loved with tender devotion, to whom he deemed himself false, and yet – could it be possible, the paradox of it? – true as the sun to the earth? The girl who had fallen into his arms and his heart like a bright, uncertain star – had she not encouraged him? Was she not a pure, innocent girl, alike as ignorant as incapable of deception? And yet – she despised him. Jeered at for his enforced desertion of his wife, a mistaken action adduced as evidence of cruelty on his part. His sensitive nature wounded in its inmost core, he lay till the early morning hours, unconscious of time or surroundings, feeling only the sad struggle and woe within him.

About daylight exhausted nature closed the weary eyelids, and he fell into a heavy but miserable sleep.

"Say, Will," shouted Tommy in his ear, all unconscious of last night's stormy ending, "breakfast's ready and you ain't up, and father's done the chores. Eat too many stolen candy sticks, maybe?"

From this child an added blow! How it struck him on his quivering nerves as he awakened with a wide sense of unhappiness. The sunshine and morning, however, seemed to restore, at least, his dignity and pride, and he answered Tommy with a sorry attempt in an answering jest.

As he hurriedly arose, under the brisk wordy shower thrown at him by Tommy, he almost smiled to find his hands full of the soft, black curls, torn so ruthlessly from his head in his last night's agony. Ah, well! His head and heart must learn to be tougher, he told himself. Misguided youth! Not tougher, but stronger.

The day dragged wearily away. When the evening came and the whole family were assembled, the young man purposely sought the side of Rhoda, with a sort of a desperate courage, that he might have a knowledge past doubt that she in truth had changed in her feelings.

Pretty, proud, offended Rhoda treated him with the airs of an offended duchess. To a student of life, her very assumptions bespoke the state of her heart; but Willard saw nothing below the haughty glance, heard nothing but dislike in the cold monosyllables vouchsafed in answer to his several questions.

After those first few days subsequent to the quarrel, he never intruded his words or his presence on Rhoda. At intervals he fancied he detected a softening in her manner, a feeling of repentance, as it were, for her former coldness. However, he knew it could only be a sickly sort of pity she would feel, anyway, and he did not care to accept cold sympathy where he once felt he had known love. So the days and weeks drifted on.

In the latter part of August, one day, the Bishop volunteered to go with him after the load of hay he intended bringing up. Together they jogged down the State Road on the hayrack, and as always Willard listened with keen pleasure to the wise, fatherly talk of the elderly man.

The talk drifted – the Bishop alone knew how – into the sea of affections, with its shoals of misunderstandings, hidden rocks, and reefs of disappointments and deceit, and its only known chart of sad experience and trial. Scarcely intending it, the young man confided to this true friend one of his secret, gnawing sorrows. What was to become of him and his life? Because his wife had chosen to desert him, must his life be forever barren?

"Have you ever read the law of Celestial Marriage, Brother Willard?" inquired the Bishop.

"No, sir, I have not. The Elders, in answer to my inquiries on the subject, while in the world, told me they were not authorized to teach that or any of the more advanced principles of the gospel; but that God would manifest the truth to me in His own time and way. To be candid, I have thought little about it. My own feelings are, perhaps, molded on the same lines as my prejudices, and it does not seem to me necessary or right for one man to usurp to himself the right to be the head and dictator of as many as he chooses."

The Bishop smiled.

"Brother, we will take up this subject at another time. Meanwhile, I advise you," speaking in his peculiar way, "to get the Doctrine and Covenants, read that revelation, ponder it well and ask God to give you the testimony of His Spirit concerning it."

They rode along in silence for a few moments; then the Bishop said.

"Sister Sarah is going to move down to the new house next week. She has no son, and I fear I can't spare any of the boys to the new house next week. Of course, there will be a hired man, Brother Mattison, but he is fresh from Denmark, does not understand the language and will not be very competent. I shall be back and forth often, but I want someone I can trust to be a help and comfort to her. She is not very strong, and needs a man to do the heaviest work. Now, my mind has rested some on you, Brother Willard, what do you say?"

How refreshing to Willard's lonely thirsting soul was this implicit confidence! With almost a quiver in his voice, he thanked the good Bishop and accepted the offer.

Thus is was settled. In the peaceful, quiet farmhouse, with kind, thoughtful Aunt Sarah, Willard settled down to something which, if it might be termed dull peace, was better than stormy unrest.

Part VI

Nothing could exceed the comfort and peace which settled down on the soul of Willard Gibbs the first night that he slept in the neat little bedroom off the kitchen which Aunt Sarah's careful hands had prepared for him. As Aunt Sarah had no boys, this room was to be his own.

With pleasure he disposed the few books that belonged to him in the two shelves which he had made at odd moments. Here, he decided, he should forget all that uneasy rapture which marked all his associations with the pretty, willful Rhoda Mainwaring. Here too he would bend his mind to fasting and prayers, that his dear wife might be brought to see the story and truth of the gospel. In this quiet, peaceful retreat, he would diligently store his mind with every good and gracious thing that was at his command. How earnest was his prayer of thanksgiving to God on this his first evening at the farm!

The intense stillness of every thing but the piercing, sweet song of the meadow lark next morning was an ample assurance that he was away from the noisy, crowded, city home of the Mainwarings. He sprang from his bed with a joyous determination to do the very best for his kind employer and friend that was in his power to accomplish.

"Aunt Sarah," he said, as they sat down at the breakfast table, with the feeling of peace still brooding over him, "I believe I shall be better and more contented here than I have been since I left my home in Virginia. There is such a spirit of quiet and comfort here."

"Did your bed lay good? You know new straw is generally lumpy and rolly; but I did the very best I could, considering I am a poor broken-backed creature," she added jokingly. "It's not always handy to have to be man, woman, and hired girl in one. But you know, I am used to that sort of thing. Women are called the weaker vessels, but I am sure they have to do all their own part and a good deal of that which man out to do. Goodness knows, though, I don't complain, for all I have never been blessed with a boy; some folks have all the boys and all the blessings and none of the drudgery, while others slave and toil without rest or change. No man ever knows what a woman endures carrying in beds and lugging round from morning till night; not but what I always enjoy working for those I love, no matter how tired I may get. I just enjoyed fixing up your room yesterday. Did you see what Ethel did? She just begged to fix up your curtains with some ribbon, so I let her have her own way. It is good to have a little help from any source; for I am such a miserable creature half the time, and beds to be filled without anyone to help you move a thing."

Just here it dawned on Willard that he had acted the part of the brute to be so inconsiderate of a frail, delicate woman like Aunt Sarah, so he began a hurried apology, with accompanying assurance of future good conduct, and begged her to call on him at any moment for all services that she might desire. He should consider it a great pleasure to wait upon her as an own son might. Kind Aunt Sarah accepted his apologies and offers with the small consciousness that she had said anything to call forth either the repentance or promise of future services. Her soft, monotonous voice went smoothly on, without break or pause, and taught by experience, Will went on about his work leaving the good lady in the middle of a sentence, explaining how utterly devoid of rest her night had been on account of baby's croupy, constant cough. He knew, if he waited to hear the last of Miss Baby's wonderful ailments and miraculous recoveries, he would have to postpone the digging of the well to some remote period of futurity.

He could not help smiling as he recalled Tommy's definition of Aunt Sarah's peculiarity, "She had discovered and applied the secret of perpetual motion in her tongue."

That evening Willard brought out a magazine and, sitting down by the center table, asked Aunt Sarah if she would like him to read to her while she worked. She accepted the offer with alacrity and at once drifted off into a detailed explanation of her intense love for literature and the depths on unhappiness she had suffered in not being able to gratify her desires; he saw he was likely to be swamped on the swift-running sea of her gentle eloquence, so at a favorable opportunity he began his reading, Aunt Sarah's voice dying away gradually in the greater volume of his own deep musical tones.

The evening passed quietly away and about ten o'clock he closed the book and said something about bedtime, but as he arose to go, Aunt Sarah asked, "Aren't you going to have prayers, Brother Gibbs?"

"Shall I?" he asked in surprised reply.

"I should think you would," she answered. "You are the man of the house here, and I am sure that the Bishop would expect you to do so."

"If you think so, then we will have prayers." And with a throbbing heart the young man made his first public prayer. It was a very halting one, but it was sincere and reached the Throne of Grace as effectually as a more elaborate one would have done.

The days passed quietly on, too quietly, poor Willard began to think, for he found the task he had set himself to accomplish was much harder than it would have been had he been in the midst of excitement and crowds. The hungry longing that assailed him to see and be near Rhoda grew more intense as the days went on. To him, with all his preconceived notions of fidelity to the wife of his youth, this was a humiliating admission. He had been taught that it was a sin for a man to love any other woman unless death severed the tie between the wedded couple. Now he found himself as deeply in love with this pretty Mormon girl as he had been with his wife before marriage deepened the bond. But why was it so? Had the separation from his wife left his heart empty? No, a thousand times no. He loved her as deeply as ever and longed for her sweet presence as before. And yet – and yet – what was the explanation of this mystery? The stories of horror he had listened to in the east came back to him with wearying persistence. Could it be possible, the devil whispered, that the very air of this territory was demoralizing?

Day after day these things came to him with increased force. Sweet, horrible suggestions of trying to win Rhoda's love and flying the country began to present themselves to his bewildered senses. What need to follow the many sad thoughts that beset him in this trying time? For such things are none too pleasant to contemplate.

One evening toward the close of the month of September he sat thinking in his own room when suddenly the saying of President Young came to his mind with all the force of spoken words, "Whenever I feel the least like praying, then is the time I need to pray the most." What comfort he had derived from that same principle once before, and why had he not thought of it now? He recalled with vivid remembrance the fact that his prayers had been singularly brief and formal of late. He had been too absorbed and too wretched to pray. Indeed, for a week past he had let his private prayers go entirely, thinking that the praying he did in the family sufficient for all purposes. Without a moment's delay, as was his own impulsive way, he locked his door and at once went down on his knees to ask God to help him out of the mental fog into which he had drifted. Cheered and comforted, he arose and went out to his dinner with a brighter air than he had worn for a month. Aunt Sarah, who was a keen observer when her own woes lifted a little, said, "You haven't heard from your wife, have you, Brother Gibbs? You look quite happy, and there is nothing like love letters to make anyone joyful, unless it is a visit instead. Do you hear from her often?"

"Not often, but occasionally."

"And how is she?"

"Oh, quite well the last time I heard from her," he replied. Then, quickly, lest she should interrupt him, he asked her, "Aunt Sarah, will you allow me to ask you a very personal question?"

"Why of course I will; ask anything you like. I am never ashamed to answer any question about myself or my life."

"How is it that women can ever content themselves to be wives of a man, knowing that his affections are centered in his first wife?"

Poor Aunt Sarah was completely astounded. Never before in her life had she felt so utterly at a loss for a word. She sat for a moment staring at her interlocuter with her mouth open but silent in dumb surprise. "What on earth do you mean?" she burst out at last. "Do you suppose that Mr. Mainwaring married me without any affection for me? Do you imagine that he thinks any more of either of his wives than he does of me? What a question to ask a good, faithful, affectionate wife!" and dissolved in a flood of tears at the very imputation, she still hurried along with questions left unanswered and answers to unasked questions, till Willard was almost beside himself with chagrin and distress.

"Please forgive me," he managed to say earnestly in a little lull of the fast-flowing river; "Don't be angry," he pleaded, "remember how ignorant I am in these matters, and I am earnestly seeking information. Therefore I sought your counsel, knowing you must understand all these matters."

Mollified as much, shall it be confessed, by the compliment as by the young man's evident contrition and ignorance, Aunt Sarah began at once to preach a gospel sermon; and, in truth, let it be said, that few could have so well discharged the task he had required. Given a principle of the gospel, an interested listener, and she was at her best. Perhaps the worthy Bishop had some such thought in his mind when he sent Willard down to the farm. He knew that his last wife was as sound on the doctrines of the Church and was withal as faithful and trustworthy a woman as there was to be found in Utah. Be that as it may, Willard, for the first time, heard with understanding ears the doctrine of plural marriage.

All the various phases of the principle were set before him: the bringing forth of a righteous seed; the refusal of women of Christian nations to bear children; the vital necessity of there being some channel opened through which the numerous spirits now waiting for a tabernacle might come and take tabernacled bodies, these spirits having been reserved to come forth in these last days; the strength and beauty of character gained by men and women by living in this order; the lifting of the curse placed on woman; and, above all, the command of God that it should be so.

"But," interposed Willard, "how can it be virtuous and proper?"

"You can see no impropriety in a man marrying one wife?"

"Of course not," laughed Willard.

"Then if he married two or more with the consent and good will of all concerned, how can there by anything immoral about it? Mind, there must be as sacred an observance of the laws of virtue and chastity as there is in monogamy. A husband must keep himself as far above the suspicion and wrong-doing as the wife must be true to the man who has her vows of fealty. Plural marriage is as far from promiscuous love as heaven is above the earth."

"Then there is no design to gratify a man's base passions that is at the bottom of the whole thing?"

"You must have paid small attention to the beautiful laws of nature that are as necessary to the highest development of the race as are the laws of horticulture applicable to the rearing of perfect flowers and fruits. No one thinks it at all impure to master every detail of the budding and cultivation of plants, the sweet mystery of the dainty pollen and its fertilization are reverently approached; but when one begins to question the attributes of man's human organization, its tender mysteries and miracles, behold, one hears the ancient cry of unclean, unclean. What a mockery! You speak of the grandest function of manhood, the point wherein he most nearly touches the divinity of his Maker, in the lowest terms. I grant that Satan and his corruption have dragged this divine attribute down to the lowest depths of perdition, and the gospel of Christ has come to us to teach us that the various parts of our natures are designed to raise us to eternal glory, and just in proportion to their strength are they most capable of raising us to heaven or lowering us to hell. The passion or attribute you have spoken of is the strongest in the human being, and illustrates perfectly my meaning. If suffered to run riot, it will sink men to the lowest depths of infamy; if honored, it serves to bring heavenly joy, peace, honor, earthly and eternal. Thus —"

At that moment baby Mary gave one of her sudden, unearthly yells, indicative of some need, and with an answering scream Aunt Sarah ran to the rescue. There could be no more talk that night as baby was a remorseful tyrant, and after prayers Willard retired to his own room. He had much to think of: a woman had talked to him on this subject with a freedom never before assumed to him even by his own mother, yet it had been done with so much dignity, in such pure language, and with so much delicate firmness, that he had felt a deeper reverence for Aunt Sarah than he ever before deemed it possible to feel for any other woman not his mother. Such new thoughts she had put into his mind. It would be wearying and needless to follow the young man through all the devious wanderings of that wakeful night.

The next morning at an early hour he was up and at his work. His hard thinking did not prevent his hard working. The noon hour came quickly and he was surprised to hear the familiar sound of the bell.

Stopping at the well for a drink of cool water, he had just raised the dipper to his mouth when a girlish figure stepped to the door and a winsome voice called out, "How do you do?"

Never till that moment did he realize the all absorbing love that filled his heart for the girl who spoke so unexpectedly to him. His heart throbbed so violently that he leaned against the well curb for a momentary support.

"When did you come down?" were the matter-of-fact words that he spoke. He was glad that she passed into the house, allowing him to go to his room and make some slight changes in his toilet before going in to speak to them all. Aunt Mary, Rhoda, Moroni, and Tommy had come down in the old carryall to spend the day. The greetings were warm and full of raillery and jest.

Aunt Sarah stood in the middle of the front room, her soft voice filling in every interstice of conversation with accounts of every known and unknown woe she had borne since the last meeting. Rhoda had assumed charge of the dinner and was flying about the kitchen with starry eyes of excitement and bright red cheeks.

"How have you been getting on, Brother Gibbs, since you deserted us?" asked Aunt Mary.

"Oh," interposes Aunt Sarah before Willard can reply, "we have had lovely times. Willard says he never was so happy or satisfied since he got to Utah. You see, we have been so quiet and peaceful, no one to torment nor tantalize, not a soul to lie around and be waited upon, though, goodness knows, I have felt as if it would be heavenly to give up and be waited on; and I guess Willard has been glad to get away from such tearing romps and tomboy rumpuses as he was obliged to witness up at the city."

"How's that, Aunt Sarah?" he asked in some surprise.

"Didn't you tell me how you enjoyed the quiet of the farm in contrast to the noise of the old home?"

Certainly he remembered saying something of that sort, but he could not for the life of him recall all that had been imputed to him. But dismissing it for the present as his memory was not ready to furnish him with his exact words, and leaving Aunt Sarah telling a long story about the good times they spent in the evenings reading, though as she spoke he could recall but one night so spent, he hurried into the kitchen to speak to Rhoda. Evidently she had heard Aunt Sarah's fling about the tomboys, and quite as evidently she thought him the originator of the remark. Her sweet graciousness of manner, the half tender glances of the eye were all supplanted by a coldness and assumed indifference of manner that completely deceived poor Will, so little did he read or comprehend the complexity of a woman's heart.

"How have you been getting on?" was his first inapt remark.

"Oh, splendidly," was the defiant reply. "Rufus Willis and Lovina and Marin Wells and I were at the big ball in the theater. You ought to have been there, it was just lovely! Father took us all out to Salt Lake last week when the President and his family were out there. We were the only others there but President Wells' family. Of course Rufus and Martin were there. Have you ever been there? It is a lovely trip to make."

Will stood looking at the dainty figure flying around the kitchen, his own hands thrust into his pockets, his moody eyes following her as she worked, and his moodier thoughts busy with the pictures of enjoyment in which he could have no part. Then the folks crowded into the kitchen as the dinner was just ready, and evidently continuing her remarks, Aunt Sarah said, "I was just telling the folks about our talk on plurality, Willard. He is the happiest mortal you ever saw on the days on which he hears from his wife. His heart is true to Poll," she laughs at her ill timed joke then. "I can tell you, girls, there is no hope for any of you. He is one of the kind that love once love forever; and he just scorns the idea of a man loving a girl when he has a first wife. If he ever asks a girl to have him, it will be from a sense of duty, from a feeling of pity for the unlucky girl," the last remark accompanied with a somewhat significant glance at Rhoda's burning cheeks. The girl felt it in a moment, and with an admirable control over her voice laughed.

"What an unlucky girl that would be, Aunt Sarah. Brother Gibbs should remember that Mormon girls marry men whose characters they know and respect. His best chance will be to convert the wife so dear to him. He might be reminded if he sought a wife in Utah, be she of ever so silly a temperament, of the famous recipe of cooking a missionary in the Fiji Islands, 'first catch your man;' but no doubt he is as indifferent to the girls as they are to him."

The cruel blow stunned him. He had said nothing, done nothing to call all this misery down upon his head. Dimly he felt that Aunt Sarah, Rhoda, and the whole Mainwaring family were against him in some sort of horrible, mysterious conspiracy to render his life not worth the living. Aunt Sarah's gentle, swift tones rarely gave anyone time to interrupt or explain. She had in some inconceivable way twisted his words and meaning, yet he realized how impossible it would be to straighten matters out.

He excused himself after dinner and returned to his work. His whole soul revolted at the bitter, undeserved taunts thrown at him by the girl he loved, and the revulsion of feeling left him stranded high and dry on the shifting sands of hatred.

Part VII

It is customary in the modern novel to portray love as the sole aim and end of a human being's existence. This is false and pernicious. Love, like ambition, is one of the strongest passions of the heart; both are susceptible of cultivation into the highest and noblest attributes, while either may be dragged in the mire of self-indulgence, becoming thereby the eternal damnation of anyone who allows the passion the guiding reins. All passions of the heart are the germs of the divinity within us. Then how kindly does our Father lead us up through tribulation to understand and appreciate the power for pure happiness within us.

The fall of 1859 was a somewhat sad time for Willard Gibbs as he felt all the intense longing for his wife and unknown babe that he had ever felt, and besides a desire to see and talk with Rhoda Mainwaring that sometimes overcame even his strong determinations; and what was hardest to his proud, sensitive and as yet ignorant spirit, he felt all the worldly shame at the two loves which in spite of himself filled his soul. He told himself over and over that he would not even try to understand the principle of plurality of wives until he could approach the holy altar unspotted by selfish motives.

Another common error of novels is the stress laid upon a circumstances in which the hero or heroine is made to suddenly alter the character or habits of a lifetime in order to produce a dramatic effect. The observations of many years have convinced me that rare indeed are the occurrences that instantaneously work changes in any man's life or disposition. It is the little, daily happenings, that, like the oft-quoted drops of water, swell the mighty torrent sweeping on to the eternal shore of destiny. To be sure there are rare earthquakes, but they only come to the occasional spots of earth, and seldom then.

So with my dear friend Will. He lived through the fall of '59, as I have said, in a miserable fashion. When he grew starved for news of his absent wife, a season of earnest prayers would leave him comforted and at peace. He noticed, too, that after one of these struggles with the Lord in mighty prayer he would soon get a letter from his faithful friend Oscar. He allowed himself no quarter as far as Rhoda was concerned, for not only was his feeling wrong for her, as he looked at the matter, but it was a matter for scorn to the little maiden herself as told by Aunt Sarah, and he was not sufficiently acquainted with womankind to understand either Rhoda or Aunt Sarah, only as he might learn by bitter and sad experience. Added to all this, he remembered his vow on his first entrance into the

Mainwaring family, and felt sorely ashamed to know how nearly he had broken his pledge. However, like the weak mortal that he was, he sometimes gave way to the desire burning within him to see the saucy face of Rhoda, and at such times he would invent or seek some excuse and, riding up to the city, spend an hour or so in the old home, carefully avoiding any special attention to Rhoda.

These visits grew rarer, and he felt as the fall wore into winter that he was gaining the coveted control over his heart. He took great interest in the letters he received from his friend in the east, not only on account of the occasional word from his wife, but he was deeply interested in the rumors of war which grew thicker and thicker. In one of his letters to Oscar he ventured to ask him if he thought his wife would accept a letter from himself. The answer was in Oscar's own generous spirit:

"Try, my dear boy, and then you will know for yourself. I broached your name to Hortense the last time I was in the old home, but she grew so angry and spoke so sharply to me for my desire to meddle in that which was none of my business, that I hastily retreated from the subject. She is well and seems to be in her usual good spirits. The boy is the one passion and ambition of her devotion. At this same visit I one day had the boy on my knee and began telling him something about his absent father, but I had scarcely spoken two words when Hortense came up behind me and, snatching the child out of my arms, commanded me to desist. She said she wished him never to hear his unworthy father's name. I asked her if she thought he would not grow up and despise her for her selfish conduct? She replied that she would rather have him die than see his father's face. This made me angry, and I retorted that the time might come when she would be too glad to see the face of her deserted husband; upon which, with a tone and manner so icy and intense that, old sceptic that I am, it made the cold chills run down my back, she answered that she should have to be dragged through the very jaws of death before she would consent to behold the face of the man who had wrecked her life. I tell you all this not to hurt your sensitive heart, for I can easily imagine how keenly it hurts, but that you may know for yourself how things are here. Still, if you care to try, write yourself; women often say things they don't half mean. But under any circumstances, rely on me as your true friend. I saw enough that terrible night in your deserted home when I came to shoot daylight through you to know that you are misunderstood, and I will not be one to throw away a friend because of a mistake in judgment.

"Instead of trying to keep you posted on all the important events that are now taking place in the South, I have begun to forward you my copy of H——'s Weekly so you can see for yourself how things go. Politics are at fever heat, you may be sure, and I dread with a horrible foreboding the events of the next year. You know how intensely Southern all our people are in their feelings, while I, either from constant association or from my Republican principles, am as intensely interested in the North. Between you and me, I think there is good and bad on both sides. Anyway, I look forward with a great deal of dread."

The newspapers came pretty regularly after this letter, and Willard read every word, even to the advertisements. The news of his wife's continued coldness was a sore trial, and he sometimes felt so discouraged that he could scarcely find hope enough to pray for her future acceptance of the gospel.

When Will answered this letter of Oscar's, he told him of the prophecy made by the Prophet in the year 1832 and quoted at length the 87th Section of the Doctrine and Covenants, in which the following occurs: "Verily thus saith the Lord concerning the wars that will shortly come to pass, beginning at the rebellion of South Carolina, which will eventually terminate in the death and misery of many souls." He also told his friend that he had decided to leave his wife in the hands of God for the present at least. He asked him, however, to keep him informed as to the health and well being of the two he held so dear, adding,

"I am glad that I am not in the east, for my very soul revolts at the thought of brother rising against brother, and if I were there I should be on the opposite side to yourself, and the misery of a chance meeting on the field of death, it is horrible to think of. This is not from any feeling of cowardice, I know you will understand that, but a feeling of human dread to shed the blood of any man. I enclose in this letter some of my hair, that you may see what an old man I am getting. I find gray hairs are quite common in my black locks."

The winter grew in severity, and the many hours of leisure left Willard at liberty to make a serious study of that much thought-of principle, plurality of wives. He prepared his heart as humbly as he could, and now that he felt he had conquered the wish to make Rhoda Mainwaring the object of his conversion to this principle, he put his whole to the understanding of the revelation. As the winter merged into spring Willard grew a little impatient and was conscious of a desire to begin to look about for himself. He had been in the Territory nearly three years, and as yet he had made nothing for himself. A few dollars in his trunk, some books and his clothes were all he had to show for his time and labor. In this he could not find any blame to attach to his kind employer, for he knew labor was too cheap, money too scarce for him to make much in this new country at day's labor. However, he felt stirring within him a longing to have a home and to begin to make for himself some ties of love and kindred. He hardly knew how to do this as his heart was centered on the wife in the east and Rhoda was a sad if not bitter memory to him. Aunt Sarah seemed to divine his feelings, a thing Aunt Sarah had a peculiar knack for doing, and spent her peculiar wit on his need for a wife and a home. He was often pained at the odd sallies which, whether unconsciously or not, partook more of sarcasm then wit. Do you know any Aunt Sarahs? How unerring is their aim at the very core of your secret sorrow, how unsparing is their quiet fling at your weakest spot.

Poor Aunt Sarah, when the first day of spring came, she was prostrated on a bed of serious illness. It happened on the 1st of March, just after Willard had gone out to his morning chores, little Ellen came running out to him and sobbed, "Oh, Brother Gibbs, come quick, mamma is dying."

Running past the frightened child, he was in the house and into the bedroom where the five little girls were all running and crying and getting in each other's way. A moment's glance showed him that the mother had fainted while trying to dress herself. He told Mary, the oldest girl, to unloose her mother's dress while he ran for water and camphor. After a few minutes, which seemed hours to the frightened group at the bedside, she opened her eyes and said feebly, "Send for the Bishop."

Then as if struck with the thought that was worrying him, she whispered, "I will manage till you return, Willard; only be quick, and ask Sister Riggs to come over as you pass her door.

Without waiting for another word he dashed out of the door, jumped on the workhorse, and with a silent prayer for Aunt Sarah's safety until he could return he sped on his way to the city. He called out to Sister Riggs, who stood outside her door, to run over to Aunt Sarah's, as she was dangerously ill. Then on to the city. The Bishop happened to be at home when Willard dashed into the yard, and a few hurried words of explanation were followed by a dash for the light wagon, Aunt Mary was told to put on her bonnet, and into the buggy jumped the Bishop and Aunt Mary. Willard rode up to the drug store for a few medicines and then followed the flying carriage.

He found the Bishop and Aunt Mary already by the sick woman's bed and came to assist the Bishop in the administration as requested. This was his first experience in this principle, and he was conscious that he was unable to exercise his faith, for he knew not how. The prayer seemed to have an immediate effect, however, for the sufferer at once opened her eyes and said feebly, "I am so glad you have come, Pa."

Meanwhile Aunt Mary moved about here and there putting things to rights, comforting the frightened little girls with assurances that mamma would soon be all right, straightening and arranging the bed, putting pillows here and there at the back and feet of the invalid, and finally at her request sitting down by the bed and soothing the restless nerves with her matchless touch.

For weeks Aunt Sarah's life hung trembling in the balance of God's hand, and what an evidence of the power of prayer was shown in her living at all. The doctor who came once to see her said frankly that he could do nothing for her. As he paused, Aunt Mary, who stood near, said quietly, "Then how great a testimony of God's power will be shown in her recovery."

"Do you think, Mrs. Mainwaring, that she is going to live?" queried the little old man who had almost studied himself into atheism.

"To be sure I do. I know she will live," was the calm answer.

"Well," he replied, "I wish you would have as much faith in my skill as you do in an unknown God. I might cure her myself if you would have such infinite trust in my skill. Faith in medicine and the one who administers it is indispensable to perfect a cure."

"But there is only a possibility of your curing her even if I trusted your skill ever so implicitly, while there is absolute certainty of her being healed if we put our whole reliance on God. Shall we not choose the surety?"

"Well, well, you Mormons are a peculiar people, no encouragement for skilled doctors or lawyers. When this woman recovers, as I suppose she will, you seem so certain about it, just let me know. It will be another evidence of the power a blind faith in an unknown and impossible God can exercise over disease and death. Singular, I must investigate the matter to the fullest extent." Then bidding them a hasty good-bye, the little doctor hurried away, muttering as he went, "Is it mind or is it will power, or is it the power of intelligence over inanimate matter? What a remarkable people, so simple-minded, and yet so wise after all."

As soon as the doctor was well out of sight, Aunt Mary took his pills and phials, and with a set look about her face she emptied them all in the stove.

The sick woman had followed her movements and, when all was thrown away, she sighed contentedly and whispered, "You are not going to leave me then, Aunt Mary, are you, until I am well? I shall soon be better if you will stay by me and pray for me all the time."

"No, Sarah, I shall not leave you till you are safe and out of danger." Then the days grew into weeks, and out of the very arms of death came poor Aunt Sarah. What a lesson of infinite love and patience did Willard draw from the faithful labors of blessed Aunt Mary. Her days and her nights were spent in constant work and prayers for the sorely afflicted Sarah. But in all her nursing and care she utterly refused to use any medicine. Nothing but the simplest teas and the mildest foods.

One day when Sarah was very low, Willard ventured to say, "Don't you think, Aunt Mary, that some quinine or some iron and quinine would rally her strength and help to bring her back to life?"

"Willard, when you have had more experience in this gospel, you will be willing to believe that our Father knows just what He is talking about. And when he says for us to nurse our sick with mild food and herbs, and that, too, not by the hand of an enemy, He means every word of it. Now I do not call such things mild, and there is a great struggle with Satan as it is for this woman's life, so I am going to give her every advantage. If pa's faith were like mine, we would give her nothing but consecrated oil and the administration of the Elders. But he has some of the old worldly notions still clinging to him, and he likes to feel we are doing something tangible for her. So I am willing to humor his notions and keep on giving her simple remedies. And at the same time I know if he would just throw away everything and depend solely upon the Lord, it would be but a few days before she would be well. You know, it is like a pair of crutches, if you insist on walking on crutches after your leg is healed, your muscles will be very much longer in getting their tension. So we are keeping Aunt Sarah on crutches, when by casting them away she would soon be able to walk alone."

All this was strange and new to Willard, and he had much to ponder over and pray over. Events transpired just as Aunt Mary predicted: slowly Sarah arose from her bed, but she did arise, much to the astonishment of the sceptical Doctor. It was June, however, before she stood once more at her door and felt the bright sunshine fill her with the smile of God's visible presence. That day, for the first time, since she came so hurriedly down to the farm, Aunt Mary took a trip to the city. Lovina had come down to stay with Sarah and the children, and Willard drove the buggy to the city.

"Aunt Mary," he said, "I have learned some wonderful things since I came to Utah. I could not have believed it possible that one woman could be so fond of her husband's wives as you all are of each other. Why no one, not an own sister, could have been more tender or watchful than you have been of Aunt Sarah. How is it? I knew Aunt Sarah loved all of you folks, but I kind of thought that was because she was so big-souled and so unselfish."

Aunt Mary smiled; how quickly she detected the Aunt Sarah flavor in that remark. "Did you fancy that she was any more unselfish than we were?" The tone was so gentle that the question was robbed of any annoyance the words might have implied. But Willard was instantly conscious of the implication of his own remark and covered with consequence confusion. How on earth did he ever get such an idea? It was more than he could tell, but the wise woman at his side knew, and with her own sweet, forgiving tact, at once forgave the inspirer of the sentiment, and set herself quietly to help the young man out of his difficulty.

"I don't wonder you are more acquainted with Aunt Sarah's kindly feelings and unselfish ways, for you have had the best of opportunities of knowing the very depths of her good disposition. But if you were as well acquainted with the rest of us, you would see we are all striving to do the very best we can. There never was a better woman than Aunt Fanny, you would soon grow to love her if you once penetrated the crust of her thorny character. Indeed we are as happy and loving a family as ever lived on earth. No own sisters could think more of each other than we all do."

"And yet you all, I suppose, have faults and sometimes have misunderstandings and even disagreements?"

"To be sure we have. Don't all own sisters have the same? Don't I see the faults of my own sisters quite plainly? Yet I love them, and would make any sacrifice for their comfort that I could."

"But it is hardly the same with the wives of one man as with the children of one parent."

"Perhaps hardly the same, but it is on the same principle. Like sacrifices have to be made of one's rights or supposed rights, and the same forgiving forbearance has to be exercised in order to live together in peace and love. Because these sacrifices have to be made, is that any reason that there shouuld be but one child, lest there should be unhappiness in the house?"

"A man's love for his wife is not like the love of parents for their children nor does the love of a wife partake of the reverence of a child for its father. I can scarcely see the force of your argument."

"You are quite right, but I was not drawing my parallel between the two lovers you speak of, but showing that it is possible for women to cultivate the same sweet graces of character in a polygamous home as in the relationship of sisters. The gain to their own nobility is quite as potent, also, as when their charity is developed by a sisterly forbearance. To answer your last remark, or rather the spirit of it, let me tell you one thing, that it is the curse upon women that their desire shall be to their husband and he shall rule over them. We want to love our husband as he loves us: tenderly, faithfully, honorably. But without that clinging to his sleeve that has been our dependence and our curse. Poets have made this cruel helplessness a model for all to copy. But we are trying to bring ourselves up out of the slough of imbecility. We want to be happy when with our husband, and not incapable of content when he is away. It may not seem possible to you now, but let me tell you and never forget what I say, that novels, poetry and the old traditions of the world notwithstanding, love is not the chief end and aim of existence. Honorable love and honorable marriage are vital necessities to every man and every woman. They can in no other way fulfill the design of their creation. But, Brother Gibbs, there are so many just as important laws for us to keep, so much work for the Saints to do. The world to warn, the dead to redeem, Zion to build up, and the great labors connected with the redemption of Israel to accomplish. Just think of it, it makes one grow dizzy to gaze upon the prospect!"

"What can a man do, Aunt Mary, who has no home, no wife, no anchor to his heart and feelings? To work well, one's heart should be satisfied and at rest."

"How truly you speak. No man can begin his life work until his soul is complete by having a wife or wives sealed to him. That is his first, most important duty. Be sure of that. Every work radiates from the home as the light radiates from the sun."

"But, Aunt Mary," how his heart beat lest she should detect the subtle meaning in his words, "what if a man loves one who is an unattainable possession, then what is he to do?"

"Ask God to help him to overcome the hopeless passion and to guide him to some faithful heart that will be a comfort and a blessing. That would be my advice to any such man." Either Aunt Mary was quite ignorant of the thought in the heart of the young man, or she wished to give him a word of timely warning that his last faint hope must die. Which ever it was, Willard accepted it as the very final burial service, as it were, over his dead love. And henceforth, sweet Rhoda Mainwaring was to be a friend or a sister to him.

One last question, "Say, Aunt Mary, what's a fellow to do who neither likes any girl, nor has a chance of making a girl love him?"

"I don't believe any such man lives in this kingdom; there is a wife or wives ready and waiting for the man who proves himself worthy of her or them."

"Then you do not think that every man should go into polygamy?"

"Not by any means. President Young says that the principle will be apt to damn more men than it will save. I think so too, for men are so careless of those sacred obligations. But when it is lived as it should be, it will exalt men and women to the highest glory. A man should first be sure that he is keeping every law of the gospel, then he can with a degree of safety enter into that great principle. If he is slack in the other laws and commandments, I don't see how he can fancy he will be strong enough to live this highest and hardest law to keep."

"Tell me, Aunt Mary, you are so wise, how can I coax a girl to have such a fellow as me?"

The gentle eyes turned to gaze at the face beside her, and her look rebuked him for the lightness of his words. "Willard, God has a hand in those matters, and if we are faithful, He will give us the wife or husband that He wishes us to marry."

"That is almost a fatality," he answered.

"No, not fatality, but the Divine guidance. We all have our agency, but by obeying the law of prayer and faithfulness, God will bring us up, perhaps through sore tribulation, to enjoy all the blessings he has held in store for us. Is it not worth the struggle?" Then they were at the gates of the city home, and Willard sprang out and helped Aunt Mary to alight.

"Oh mother," said Rhoda, as soon as Aunt Mary opened the door, "Tommy has just come down with the scarlet fever. And we have all been exposed. What will you do?"

"Gracious, how did he get that?"

"Caught it from the school children," answered Aunt Fanny. Adding, "I hardly think it wise for you to go away again, for I am afraid it will go through the family. How is Sarah? Is she well enough for you to leave her alone?"

"No, I do not dare leave her all alone with her children. Her girls are so silly about sickness, and they are nothing but children anyway. If I stay, we'll have to find some one to go down there for a few weeks or even a month or two."

Just here the Bishop came in saying, "I have told Willard that he had better not come in the house as he will want to go back to the farm, and I don't want to run any risks of the children down there getting the fever. Now, Mary, what is to be done about Sarah? She must not be left alone."

"That is what we have been talking about, father. I wonder if we could get Harriet Morse to go down for awhile?"

"I am afraid not," said Aunt Fanny, "she is going out to Grantsville this week."

"Who is there? Say, I wonder if one of the Lang girls wouldn't go down for awhile? Let's send Rhoda over and see. I don't believe either one is going off anywhere this summer."

Rhoda was dispatched at once to ask Sister Lang if she would spare one of her girls to help Aunt Sarah until she was strong enough to get along alone. She found the girls both at home, and both were quite willing to go. But after some talk between the mother and the girls, it was decided that Aseneth should go. She agreed to be ready in a couple of hours at which time Willard was to call for her.

Rhoda met Willard as she was going in her gate and told him he would have to wait a couple of hours. He asked her who was going down, and she replied maliciously that it was one of the girls Dame Rumor had married him to. Willard colored painfully and turned away. Why should this girl take so much delight in tormenting him? He had not merited such treatment at her hands.

The bitter thought, however, did not make the quiet bow with which he excused himself a bit less gentlemanly, nor did it make the even tones of his voice falter as he said, "I will go up to the post office, Miss Rhoda, while I am waiting; if you will be kind enough to tell the Bishop where I have gone."

At the end of the two hours Willard was at the home of the Langs, and in a very few minutes thereafter Aseneth came out and the two started down to the farm.

"What a siege of sickness Bishop Mainwaring is having this spring. First Aunt Sarah, and now scarlet fever in the family," remarked the young girl.

"It is so in all families, I reckon. Disease is no respecter of persons. Is this the first time you have been down to the farm, Miss Lang?"

"Yes the first time since the new house was built. I have been down several times to picnics years ago. In fact, last summer some of us were down here for a ride just before the building was done."

The talk drifted away to picnics and parties. I have not spent much time describing the various characters of this story; but I cannot refrain from presenting some sort of picture of this lovely girl sitting so quietly at the side of my friend Willard Gibbs. You need not fancy, because I say lovely girl, that I have strict reference to the contour of head or to the perfection of features. But there was a something about Aseneth Lang that every one who became acquainted with her characterized as lovely. The mere detail of dark hair and eyes, the smooth skin and gentle expression of her face is perhaps all the outline I can make for you. Fill in the sketch with the trait of sweet unselfishness and charity for all human things, which trait, like the clearness of a deep mountain stream, gives the charm of loveliness to all its meanderings. No one ever heard an unkind word uttered against the character of another from the lips of this carefully trained Mormon girl. She was one of those rare, noble creatures that come seldom to this sad earth. That she had faults was as certainly true; else would she not be living now as she most assuredly is. But those faults were negative rather than positive, and even the few who find it in their hearts to criticize so excellent a character can only call her weak and too forgiving. I have heard Aunt Sarah say Aseneth was never so happy as when she was being abused. That was Aunt Sarah, however, and I know Aseneth well enough to know she does not enjoy imposition any better than anyone else, but when it comes to her, she bears it with that gentle, uncomplaining spirit that our Aunt Sarah tries in vain to successfully imitate. If you would be interested in knowing how this girl bore the trials of life and the consequent effect on her character, bear with me till we shall reach the end of this, our true tale.

Aunt Sarah welcomed Aseneth with garrulous cordiality. She insisted on Willard going into the barn and removing all his clothing and bathing with other modes of purification lest he had brought a particle of the dreaded contagion along in his clothes. The fever at the town house of the Mainwarings successfully cut off all intercourse with those at the farm. Poor Aunt Sarah was weak in body and her fears ran away with her judgment. One day several weeks after Aseneth had been domiciled there, the Bishop was seen driving into the yard. Aseneth told Aunt Sarah so, and the good lady sprang to the door and hailed him.

"Oh Pa, surely you are not coming into the house when you are just down from that terrible disease. Please don't. Baby was feverish all night, and Mary has been sick for a day or two; you know how bad it is for children to be ailing anyway and then be exposed to the germs of disease. It seems impossible to keep them from catching it. Why, only yesterday the baby had a rash on her skin that almost frightened me to death. I haven't had a night's rest for a month, what with the children being sick and then my own feelings. Up and down, up and down, all night long, and me as weak as an hour-old calf. Of course I supposed 'Seneth would get up if I called her, but you know how it is with the young people. Once asleep, asleep till a cannon ball wakes them. And she likes to read so well that it is late when she gets time in the evening, and Willard –"

The Bishop had driven to the inner yard long before the close of this rapid expostulation and sat patiently listening as long as he could, but finally interrupted her, saying, "How are you, Sarah, as regards your general health?"

"Oh, as I was saying, I am not strong at all, but I manage to get around and do a good deal, for if I did not I am sure I can't see how things would go in the house. With only a girl who is not the best of housekeepers, if she is the brag of all who know her for her disposition, which goodness knows –"

The Bishop knew from the admission about the ability to get around and see after things that the speaker was much better even if she had not poured forth the full tide of her old-time eloquence; so gently interrupting her he said, "Sarah, I have some bad news to tell you. Are you strong enough to bear it?"

They were outside, and the woman leaned up against the rails as she said in reply, "What is it? Not Mary, or Fanny?" For with all her peculiarities she loved her two sister wives with even more devotion than they did her.

"No, it is not the girls, but Mary's George died this morning from the fever. The rest are all better. The 'girls' wanted me to come down and tell you myself and to say they sent their love and prayers for you and that you were on no account to think of coming up there. Mary, of course, feels terribly bad, but Lovina seems the most cut up over it. She was so fond of the little chap." The Bishop could control himself no longer, and with a groan he leaned over the gate and wept. Aunt Sarah, with a loyal desire to comfort, tried to say something to ease his grief. But failed miserably, for after one or two faltering words, she, too, burst into tears and they both cried bitterly for some moments. Perhaps, after all that was the best comfort she could have given him, for a broken heart feels no sympathy so keenly as the silent sympathy of mutual tears.

You have become little acquainted with the Bishop if these tears of his causes you a moment's surprise, for he was one of the tenderest-hearted men alive, and tears were as much a relief as were Aunt Sarah's own. To be sure, they did not fall so often, nor were they so near the surface, but they came sometimes, and when they did the man was wise enough to thank God that he could so relieve the tension of his over-charged heart.

Aunt Sarah sent a dozen loving messages and said she would send Willard with the two-seated wagon to be there at the funeral, adding, "But don't, above all things, let him go in the house, or let him take any of the folks from the house out to the grave; there will be plenty of carriages, so just let him take some of the friends instead of our folks. You don't blame me for being careful; I feel to be so more than ever, don't you?"

The Bishop promised to remember all she had charged him with, mighty as would be the task.

The next day at an early hour the carriage was hitched up and Willard came into the house for the messages he had always to deliver. He found Aseneth all ready to go along, and listened in respectful silence to the interminable instructions and interdictions Aunt Sarah poured out. Suddenly she seemed to remember something, and without cutting off her discourse, she drifted into one of her odd, mirthless laughs and said archly, "Now you two young people ought to manage before long to bring that story so often told about you true. There is nothing to hinder it, so far as I know; I was just telling 'Seneth the other day that she would –"

What all she had told Aseneth did not then transpire, for, like the quick, impulsive lad he was, the sting of mortified pride in Willard's heart was communicated to his hands, and the horses sprang off at a run with the lash of the whip they had felt on their backs, leaving Aunt Sarah to give one scream of fright and dismay at the dangerous position she had been in, and then turn into the house with an inward congratulation to think she had been so clever as to get in her little joke and hint all in so few words and at such a time. As for one of the victims of her ill-placed pleasantry, he felt as if he was doomed to be hurt by those he loved best. With it all he felt sulky and disagreeable, and not for worlds could he have been his usual genial, gentle self to the innocent cause of all his distress. She sat, poor girl, conscious of the mortification her companion was enduring, too conscious, for it rendered her unable to be her usual sunny self, thus making it difficult to dispel the cloud between them.

On arrival at home, both Lovina and Rhoda came out and asked Willard and Aseneth at once to come in as the services were about to begin.

"You will have to excuse us," replied Willard in none too gentle a way, "we have been sent up here to look on." I am ashamed to confess that for the moment Willard had forgotten the sad occasion that had brought himself and companion there and remembered only himself and his uncomfortable position. To complete the confession, I must further say that his angry resolve to make it impossible for him to be caught in such a situation again was accompanied in his own mind with sundry expletives that were neither elegant nor hardly just to the various causes of his discomfort.

Lovina looked a little shocked at the half-angry tone of his voice, while Rhoda took no pains to disguise the disgust she felt at his words and situation. Aseneth hastened to explain how anxious Aunt Sarah was to show in some way her keen sympathy and sorrow, and as she could not possibly come herself she had sent them to be as it were her representatives, thus furnishing a couple of seats for friends who wished to go along to the "graveyard."

It was useless for Willard to remember how easily he might have avoided this scene by simply waiting until the services were well under way; nor did it add to his comfort to know that the presence of Miss Aseneth was almost as unwelcome as it was unexpected. It was enough to know that the only thing to be done was to sit there silently and respectfully until such time as he was released to go home.

The services were short, and as they neared the close, quite a number of carriages drove up to the gate, some with people who felt the same fear of contagion that Aunt Sarah did; so the two occupants of the carriage felt a little relieved to find they had so much company in their waiting. Not a word was exchanged between the two during their hour's delay, for Aseneth was a little hurt at the unnecessary sulkiness of her companion and the situation was one in which she had no hand.

The rest of the services were without incident so far as Willard was concerned, and the ride home was almost as silent as the ride up to the city. As they traveled along homeward in silence, it occurred to Bro. Gibbs that he had been acting like a boor. The quiet girl at his side, and the sudden remembrance that in all likelihood she had been as annoyed to be forced to accept his disagreeable company as he had been to accept hers made a quick glow of shame pulse through him. He was a man, and like a man thought first of his own position; but he was not a selfish man at heart, and the training of childhood was more at fault for his "manliness" in that respect than the natural disposition of the lad. So after swallowing in a measure the lump of discomfort in his breast, he began a disultory conversation on the many improvements the city had undergone since he came to its friendly gates.

The days passed at the farm in the same monotonous fashion they had always done. Willard was very anxious to make some kind of a start at a home of his own; but he hardly knew how to get away from the Bishop, and yet he felt he must.

Without any distinct utterance as to words, Willard was yet unconsciously lifting up his heart in silent and constant prayer to God for the way to be opened for him to get a home of his own; I say he did not formulate any words, he had not had the experience in those matters that older members of the Church had enjoyed. If I were to try to describe more fully what I mean, I should tell you that every time he thought about the matter, and that was very seldom, this wish would accompany the thought – "Oh that God would bless me with a house and home of my own –" but he had not thought of getting down on his knees and making it a subject of prayer. He learned the greater power given by this humble abandon of one's self to the mercy of God at a later period in his life, but as he had as yet not done so, his ignorance was not counted unto him, and the God he yearned to hear and answered his unspoken desires. At least so he expressed his view of the events that thereafter transpired.

On the first of July, the Bishop's buggy drove into the farm yard at seven o'clock in the morning. The folks had just separated for the day's work, Aunt Sarah being busily engaged in that thankless but necessary task of cleaning up children for the day. Aseneth was washing the breakfast dishes, while Willard was just driving out of the yard. The Bishop asked him to wait a few minutes and he would go along; then turning to respond to the noisy greeting of the children and to make Aunt Sarah happy by a few tender words of sympathy and a hearty kiss, the good man sat down on the doorstep and delivered his errand.

"'Seneth, there is to be a grand march in the city this Fourth, and my girls are invited to take a part. Your sister was going to be one of the marchers, but she is afraid the walk will be too much for her. Now, she wanted me to ask you if you would not take her place, and she said something about your wearing her dress. Here is a letter from her that will explain it all, I guess, better than I can. Sarah, the children are all well, and we have had everything cleaned up and there is not the least danger, so I want you to come up and bring all the children to spend the Fourth. I will come down on the third and help Willard to get you all up there. What do you say, Sarah?"

"Just what I always say, pa, I go and come as you want me to. But who all is to march? Are either of the 'girls' going?"

"I guess not, I haven't heard them say anything about it. Of course Mary wouldn't feel like it, and Fanny is not strong enough to walk in the procession."

The prospect of the holiday and the affectionate remembrance of her by all the "folks" made Aunt Sarah's heart warm with cheerful happiness, and if it was her way to show it by jokes and laughs and hints and pleasantries of various sorts, at least she had a right to her way. The bishop excused himself to her for a few hours as he wanted to go out with Willard and see how things were getting along. So after the buggy horse was put in the stable recently built by Willard, the two men drove out of the yard in the wagon and made a complete tour of the farming land now under cultivation. Then the Bishop told Willard to drive over to the "twenty-acre" piece adjoining, which as yet had never had the virgin soil turned over to the face of the sun.

"This," explained the Bishop, "I entered as part of my claim at the same time I entered the rest of this quarter section. You see, it lies kind of corner ways to mine, but it is all included in the entry I made when I first came in. What do you think of this piece? Do you like its looks and situation?"

"Why, I did not know this was yours. I have often looked at it and wondered why it was not under cultivation. It will make someone a pretty farm. I think this land right here is as good as any in this whole valley. I never saw a better crop than is growing on the field adjoining this."

"Brother Willard, what are your intentions regarding your future life? You are a good school teacher, and we greatly need teachers. Do you intend to resume your labors in that line?"

"To make an honest confession," said the young man after a moment's reflection, "I do not think I should like to make my living at school teaching. I had a good trade that earned my living before I came here, but that, too, makes a man the servant of another man as long as he works for him. I think if the chance ever comes to me I shall get some farming land and build me a home on it. I find my health is excellent down here, and I enjoy the freedom of a farmer's life. I will be frank with you, Bishop, and say that this subject has been on my mind a good deal of late, and I have longed to have a talk with you in relation to the matter, but I hesitated somewhat lest you should think I was dissatisfied and ungrateful for all your kindness to me."

"You need have no fears on that score, Brother Willard, for I understand your feelings exactly. I will say further that I have helped many a man to get a start in this city and seldom have they thought it necessary to consider my interests or to do anything but make as much out of me as they could and then go off without a word of gratitude or acknowledgment. I don't say this to find fault, for we come to these valleys filled with selfishness and ignorance. It takes some a long time to become familiar with the Holy Ghost, which is the spirit of charity and unselfishness. We think we have the spirit of our religion in the old country, or in our old home, but when we find that Zion is a temporal as well a spiritual kingdom, we let ourselves return to the old worldly thoughts and feelings. There is a great deal of every man for himself, and the devil for us all right here in Zion; but we have got to get rid of that feeling sooner or later, and I realize for one that the best way for me to help that state of things to get here is to begin with Bishop Mainwaring and his family, then help my friends and neighbors to do as I am trying to do. But there, I am preaching a sermon instead of telling what I am going to do with the twenty-acre piece; here," drawing out a paper from his pocket, "is a paper I have made out to you for a quit claim deed to this land. Now, if you would like to settle down here on this place and make you a home, I shall be very glad, for I shall feel then as if Sister Sarah will have someone always near her to be a friend and to look after her interests when I am not here. Poor girl, she has no boys, and that is a great trial to her."

Willard was unable to answer for a few minutes, then he poured out his gratitude for the kindly act, and in his heart he was far more grateful than he could tell for the tact with which the Bishop made the gift seem a help to himself. Then he asked in what way was he to make the payments for the land, for he had saved very little of the wages he had earned. Greater still was his astonishment to hear the answer.

"You need not take any thought on that subject, Brother Willard, for you are quite welcome to the land without anything to pay. But if you do well and really want to do so, you can pay me for the expense I have been to in entering and fencing the land. That is all I shall accept under any circumstances, for I am not likely to forget your devotion to me and my interests. You are a true son of Ephraim, and as such I bless you and say you shall be blessed, your land and your crops shall be blessed, your house and your home, and you shall yet receive four-fold for all that you have sacrificed for the church and kingdom of God."

Again that great promise, for the third time, had been pronounced upon his head. With no spoken word, only a glance of grateful love into the keen, kindly eyes bent on him, he turned his horses' heads in obedience to the word of the Bishop, and the elder man knew the heart of the younger one and felt a deeper affection for the homeless lad than he had ever felt before.

As they jogged quietly along, the Bishop said, "You will have to look you up a wife, Brother Gibbs. Houses are not homes without wives in 'em. No man can go alone into the celestial kingdom. Men and women are useless when separated, but of great worth when united."

"I thank you, sir, for your kind advice, but I would not know where to look for a wife. I am not as bold as some men, and I don't think I am much of a favorite with the girls."

Well, make the matter a subject of constant prayer, for it is of the utmost importance for a man to get the right one or ones. And I know of no way to do that except to get inspiration from God to know whom to choose."

They were at the farm gate, and Aunt Sarah came out to say that they had been waiting dinner for "hours."

It was arranged that Willard should go up the next day and take Aseneth, who would have a good deal of preparing for the grand march which was to come off on the Fourth. The Bishop promised to come down on the afternoon of the third to drive timid Aunt Sarah and the children to the city. With many and conflicting emotions, Willard passed the next two days.

Part VIII

"Girls, that's the cannon; it's daylight."

The the jumping and scrambling and hurrying. It was the morning of the Fourth, and the Mainwaring girls with Aseneth Lang were hastily preparing to run downstairs and help get the children ready for the day. Aseneth had been persuaded to stay all night at the Mainwaring's in order to be with them at the march.

Downstairs all was hurry and confusion. Aunt Fanny alone was as little upset by the merry uproar as she would be if nothing out of the common was going on. Nothing ever made Aunt Fanny disorderly or put out. She went on the calm tenor of her way as undisturbed by noise or other worry as a rock in a brawling stream is unfretted by the foaming waters around it. As for poor Aunt Sarah, who was not any too strong, the excitement rose in her head like bad wine, and she alternately begged her children to be still and whimpered about her inability to get them ready.

"Helen," she called to the eldest girl, "why don't you do something towards getting yourself ready. You will be behind all the rest, and who'll care if you are? You know you are not strong, and you have to get along without any help but your poor, sick, good-for-nothing mother's; land of mercy, don't cry about it," the mother's dismal forecasts had unlocked the fountain of childish tears, "it won't do any good to cry. Stand still while Aseneth combs your hair, and don't bother her with your sobs. I don't know how it is," the mother confided to Aunt Mary's kind ears, "but my Helen is so tender-hearted."

"I should think she was!" said Tommy to Willard, as the two stood washing their hands in the sink, "Helen's so tender-hearted that her mother can't ask her to get a pail of water but she has to bawl." Tommy's wink and Willard's smile were lost in the wash basin, but Aunt Sarah's quick ear caught the words, and she said plaintively:

"I don't wonder at your unfeeling cruelty, Thomas, for no one can expect anything else out of such a selfish, petted child; but the time will come when women's aches and pains will receive something more at mens' and boys' hands than ridicule. If you ever could once suffer in your back what poor Helen does in her back, you would never carry a pail of water if people choked for it." This rebuke was a very proper one for the lad, but she did not go on to tell why it was that poor Helen had such a bad back. Chronic laziness, a diet of grease, sugar, pork and coffee, with the cruelty of boned and corded waists which pinched the slender, girlish form into a perfect reflection of her mother's hour glass waist at the same age, made fifteen-year-old Helen a misery to herself and a burden to her mother.

"Say, Willard," joked Aunt Sarah, as he was combing his hair before the one glass, "you ought to take me and 'Seneth to the grand ball tonight, for we come nearest to being your folks than anyone else here."

"I have asked Miss Aseneth to do me the honor to accompany me to the ball, and include you in the invitation if you care to go," he replied calmly. It was a good thing he had already asked Aseneth, for that unlucky way of Aunt Sarah's would have made him as contrary as a "man" or a mule. Rhoda, too, had heard the reply, for she was just entering the door at the other end of the long dining room. She had a dish of hot gravy for the breakfast table, and perhaps that was the reason why her face was glowing and eyes so full of something suspiciously like tears. At any rate, no one saw the deadly paleness that followed the flush, for she had hurried out to get some kindlings. My sweet little Rhoda! How it makes my heart ache to dwell on the suffering you went through that memorable Fourth. However, there was too much to be done for her to sit down and realize how very wretched she was. What a blessing work is to the unhappy! Without it, life would be unsupportable!

The time soon came to gather in the schoolhouse, and the three girls started in good time. No prettier sight ever was seen to issue from the homely portals of that house than those three girls. Lovina, beautiful with all the wealth of her deep blue eyes, perfect features and skin of pure, flawless, white, made delicious by the tinge of delicate pink brought by excitement, she was the fairest of the three. Rhoda's piquant face was charming in its own way, and when anyone really loved her, she seemed even more pretty than her perfect sister. At least that was the somewhat sad conclusion of the young man who watched them all go out the gate with a touch of the old miserable pain. The sunny eyes of little Rhoda wore a somewhat unusual expression today, but the hidden sorrow in them only served to make them sweeter and kinder than was their wont. Aseneth looked lovelier than she ever did in her whole life. Something had brought to her face an expression of happiness and personal delight that lent the one lacking element to make her really lovely. She was at last alive. A pulsating, throbbing human being. Her unselfish disregard of her own happiness and the constant serving of everyone's interest but her own had given her a pure, chaste expression; but it was, if I could say so, a distant light shining in a far-away star. Now she seemed warmer, fuller of the same emotions that agitate other girls, and with this she seemed to be of the same earth as the other two, and the gain was an infinite one to Aseneth's attractiveness. I half believe Rhoda dimly sensed this fact, for she more than once turned to look squarely at the lively "unusual" Aseneth. They were all three dressed in white muslin dresses, made in a perfectly plain fashion, the deep hem at the bottom of the skirt being the only suggestion of ornament, unless the simple, tiny, lace ruffle at the neck and sleeves could be called ornamentation. Pink ribbons at throat and on the flowing hair, which had been coaxed into curls by Aunt Mary's deft fingers. With the cloudlike floating sashes of blue tarleton from shoulder to waist, made up the simple but becoming costumes of these fair girls. At the end of the day, you will find Lovina as delicately robed as now, not a lock out of place, not a ribbon crushed. How she will manage it I am not prepared to say, but it will be so, for I have seen her do the same way times without number. Rhoda will be a flying mass of tumbled curls, face like a full-blown rose, sash torn, and ribbons untied; but even then she will be a most charming picture for those who look with partial eyes, for her confusion is that so recklessly praised by poets, the gay disorder of a romping Hebe. While strange as it may be, Aseneth will have neither the orderly primness of Lovina, nor the sweet confusion of Rhoda. Her curls will hang limp, and her dress will be draggled, and a general air of forlorn disorder will make her greyish pale face and tumbled garments neither attractive nor even pitiful. At this moment, however, the three looked their very best, and their merry chatter made the whole air vibrate with excitement.

They had but gone out when Aunt Mary appeared in the door.

"Girls," she called, "are you going off without Helen? You know she has been hurrying to get ready to go with you."

The three paused in some shame at their thoughtlessness, and Aseneth answered, "Tell Aunt Sarah we will take good care of her, and she won't need to worry about her at all." Then on they hurried to the school house where were more girls and some young men and many children ready to take their places in the march.

Our friends are soon joining in the general chattering confusion; and, when the superintendent calls for them to take their places in the line, there is a general rush. "Lou," says Rhoda in a whisper to her sister, "walk with me, won't you?"

"Why of course, but you always want 'Seneth, so I told Jenny I would walk with her."

"I don't want to walk with her today." Lovina fancies she detects a note of pettishness in her sister's words; but she knows how quickly Rhoda is offended and thinks little of the matter.

With a good deal of shouting and changing and fluttering, the procession is formed and the march begins. The band is at the head with its perfect time and delightful music. Next are the civil officers, then the carriage garnished with a handsome flag with the Governor and the Secretary; these are followed by groups of young ladies representing the states and territories, each division with appropriate banners. Now comes the sensation of the day, a huge car in which the tallest and handsomest young woman in the country stands in the classic robes of the Goddess of Liberty. The car is decorated with the stars and stripes in profusion and is drawn by four white prancing horses. Then, the brass band follows, ringing out the brazen music alternately with the martial band. Now follows the trades represented by a man seated on a platform and at work on his trade. Various other organizations are represented in various ways, and finally the Sabbath Schools in their proper order with floating banners and flags bring up the rear of the long procession. In their own proper ward division, our three friends had their places as Sunday School pupils. Lovina and Rhoda marched together, carrying a silken banner between them. Just behind, came Aseneth and Jenny Fairbanks.

As they reached the threatre corner, they passed their own folks who had taken their stand at that place. Willard stood nearest the procession, and, as they met, Lovina gave him a smile and nodded gaily to the rest of the family. Rhoda was apparently too busily engaged in turning the banner around to see any of the folks. But the one watcher who noted her every expression saw there was a very haughty, bored look on the piquant face. Then his eye caught that of Aseneth, who smiled in her gentle, quiet way, and as he met her eyes he noticed it seemed to him for the first time those eyes were very sweet, very attractive. No thrill accompanied that observation, but he was made sensible of the fact.

The hot July sun had little mercy for anybody, and great was the joy of all when the turn was made and the whole line poured into the Temple gate and were at last seated in the cool, leafy bowery. The exercises that followed, who does not know them? The reading of the Declaration of Independence, the singing of the Star Spangled Banner, the choruses by the choir, the addresses by different societies, the speeches inciting all to loyalty by the leading brethren, and finally the reading of toasts. All interspersed by patriotic music, by martial and brass bands, and ever and anon, the booming of a cannon to mark the various divisions of the programme.

The services were all over about three o'clock, and the people hurried home to eat and rest preparatory to the grand ball to be held in the evening. The three girls returned in just the condition I predicted they would. But when they had changed their dresses for clean print ones, they were once more good to look upon.

After dinner all separated to take a couple of hours' rest, and Rhoda begged Lovina not to ask Aseneth to stay with them any longer. Lovina complied with the request, and so it happened that the two girls were alone in their own room.

"Say, Rhoda, what on earth ails you? I don't know when I saw you look and act as you have done lately," said Lovina as they were disrobing.

"Oh Lou, I am the miserablest wretch that ever lived." And the poor child threw herself on the bed with a perfect passion of sobs.

"Well, what is the matter?" asked Lou in amazement.

"I just hate that mean Aseneth Lang. I hate her; I wish I was dead!"

"What's 'Seneth been doing to you?"

"I just believe she is another Aunt Sarah with her smooth tongue and her mock-martyr airs. She makes me sick every time I look at her."

"How long have you felt this way, Rhoda?" asked her sister, who knew and loved the impetuous child beside her too well to more than wonder at this outburst.

"All day long." And another storm of sobs shook the very bed.

"Well say, Rhoda, you know I can't tell what to say to you until I know what ails you; so sit up and tell me."

"Oh it's nothing," sitting up with a poor little attempt at pride, "I suppose I am a fool, and that's the truth of the whole matter. Don't say anything about my stupid actions, will you? Don't tell mother, it worries her so. You lay down and have your sleep; I can't sleep, so I am going down to press out my dress. I will do yours too, if you like."

Lovina accepted the generous offer, and turning over to sleep she resolved to keep a little closer watch on Rhoda and find out what really ailed her.

As Rhoda passed through the upper hall, she was obliged to pass the door of the boys' room; the door was open to catch any faint breath of air that might be passing, and as she looked in she saw Willard on his low single bed in his shirt sleeves asleep; his head raised on the pillow, his arm thrown over his black, curly head, and the brilliant red lips gleaming under the dark moustache. She stood for one brief second, and the passionate heart sent to her lips one moan of the deepest agony. She would have given her very life to have dared to go in that room and lay her own bright head on that manly breast just where her tresses would meet his lips, and there sob out the love and woe that seemed to be consuming her. The sound of her low moan seemed to have disturbed his sleep, and with a restless movement he threw up both his arms with a murmured name that she could not catch. But the possibility of his awakening and finding her there sent her flying down the stairs, and she ran on down to the orchard to cool her flushed face and bathe her hands and short curly hair in the running brook.

Her early training stood her in good stead now, for jumping up into her seat in the crook of the apple tree, she laid her head down on her hands and bowed her heart in a simple, earnest prayer. Poor, sweet, passionate Rhoda, thy discipline was very hard to endure, but God knew what was best. In a few minutes the calm the prayer brought to her soul, the sultry quiet of the air, and the drowsy hum of all nature about her soothed her to rest, and she fell asleep.

When she awoke, she had barely time to iron out her finery, and Lovina had to do her own. Rhoda had very little desire to go to the ball, but even the prospect of dancing once with her heart's idol was enough to make the evening eagerly longed for. Once at the Bowery where the ball was to be held the music made her forget everything but her love for dancing. And, with a comparatively light heart, the maiden joined in the general enjoyment.

The evening was already far spent before Willard presented himself for the regulation dance. Then Rhoda was reckless enough to grant his polite request with a gay abandon of manner that puzzled her partner. As they made their way through the crowded door, she clung to his arm, and pressed close to his side, giving full reign to the delight she felt at being so near him, and chattered with heed volubility. He was puzzled and almost suspicious. Why did this girl treat him so strangely? Did she wish to play fast and loose with the deepest feelings of his heart?

Backward and forward, across and around, they danced in the old-fashioned quadrille, and all too soon it came to an end, and they turned to find their seats. As she leaned close to his ear in their walk across the room, she whispered with a quick little catch in her breath, "Oh Will, I wish that dance might last forever!"

"Do you?" he answers quietly. "What a dancer you are, Miss Rhoda." Then for a brief moment their two eyes met, and he read the pain in hers to be the distress of a wicked creature when it sees its victim slipping from its grasp, and she read the half contemptuous pity in his eyes aright, but guess nothing of its real cause. So the dance was ended for those two, and the evening was soon over for all.

Willard could not sleep much that night, for he was full of thought; and afterwards, just at daybreak, he lost consciousness in the midst of a prayer to God to give him some testimony as to whether he should try and gain the consent of Aseneth Lang to be his wife. He had no idea, of course, as to whether he should succeed if he were to try, yet he felt anxious to know the mind of his Heavenly Father before he even sought the hand of the young woman; so, as he had before learned, he determined to seek a testimony from the source of light and truth before committing himself in a single action. He felt he had been foolish once, now he would try to be wise and not have to undo what he did. All this was well, God had his heart in His hand and turned it withersoever He would!

The eastern mail that month was somewhat detained and did not reach the city until the fifth of July. But knowing it was to be in on that day, Willard remained up in town until the evening waiting for it. He was rewarded for his trouble, for the postmaster handed him a letter, directed in Oscar's handwriting, and four packages of papers. He hurried away to a quiet spot to read his letter.

"I send you the Weeklies that you may see just what a hell's pot has been set aboiling here by the firing of Fort Sumpter."

Then followed a description of the local disturbances that were opening in all directions; and of the family quarrels and bickerings that were making life a torture to every dweller in the doubtful states.

"I am almost afraid to visit Aunt Mary or mother. Mother is especially rabid in her southern proclivities. She has written me bushels of firey letters filled with Spartan mother allusions, the northern barbarians, and swords and cannons. I am positively afraid to tell her how my sympathies run, for I believe she would renounce me and even denounce me. So, like the white livered poltroon that I am, I stay here scratching down figures in the ledger when I ought to be out putting myself in trim to be something more than a burden to my country. I only wish you were here, you have no coward's blood in your veins, and if you were here, we would take our muskets and together fling away everything but duty and honor and face the greybacks."

Just here Willard sighed, for his blood boiled to be there and take part in the glorious contest for right, but he sighed for his heart was with the southern soldiers, and he knew if there he and Oscar would be on opposite sides of the field. So he thanked his luck that he was engaged in something of more weight than the fight of two great powers for might. The letter went on:

"I heard a hint of some trouble between mother and Hortense; but I reckon it is all patched up, for they are to start for Europe on the next steamer. This action on the part of my ambitious mother means something. I wrote a long letter to Hortense, carefully avoiding any mention of your name lest it might anger her again; but so far, she has not deigned me any reply. I did mention, however, something about the strange prophecy made by your Mr. Smith in relation to the Civil War. It struck me and I really thought it would interest her. Say, that was a singular thing. Tell me something about this odd man, and send some more of that quaint little weekly, the Deseret News. I was interested in reading it, and gathered some ideas about the wild country you are subduing."

Willard went immediately to get some books to send to his friend. His heart beat high with hope that his efforts to quietly preach the gospel to his beloved friend might soon bear some precious results. The purchase of several of the Church works and a whole bundle of papers made a heavy inroad on his slender purse, but he gave it with such a joyful heart that it could in no wise be termed a sacrifice. The whole package was carefully wrapped and directed, and then he turned cheerfully homeward to read his bundle of papers. The knowledge that his wife was even now across the sea was not very pleasant, but he had so far trained himself that he could commit her to the hands of God, and there let the matter rest. He should be more diligent in his prayers for her safety and the welfare of his lovely boy with an added wish that she might not be involved in any of the ambitious, unscrupulous designs of her Aunt, Oscar's mother.

The long ride down to the farm that evening after dark with Aseneth beside him was far from unpleasant. The moon was a brilliant lamp for their guidance, and as he was full of news he had received from the east, he poured out to his companion descriptions of their old home, and the condition of things that must now necessarily prevail. She was a delightful listener, full of subtle suggestions of sympathy and close interest. She seemed to know instinctively just what to ask and how to put in those little interjectionary interludes that keep a one-sided conversation from being tiresome and dull. Even his wife crept into the talk, in some unexplained way, but so gentle was the interest manifested by the girl, that before he realized how freely he was talking he spread open one whole page of his heart for this sweet sympathy so quietly offered him. Aseneth was a girl of few words, but no one knew it; she had so apt a way of making her companion do the talking about the very subject nearest his heart that he was only conscious afterwards of a glow of pleasure at the pleasant time spent, and people generally ended by calling Aseneth a very satisfactory companion.

Willard lay down that night pleased with the impression made upon him by Aseneth and mingled with that reflection was a vague hope that she would be as pleasant to him always even to the granting of nearer and dearer rights. You are not to think that my friend was of a fickle or an inconstant nature – far from it; for the loves he once took into his heart never left him entirely. But he was just like all other healthy mortals, he could not very well go on loving a shadow; and, being but a man, he could not content himself with either memories or hopes. He wanted some love and some ties of his own. God made him so, and I am not ashamed to acknowledge it. It is only in unhealthy novels that the youth goes off and becomes a misanthrope for the girl who treats him before marriage as he doubtless would after marriage have treated her. To be sure, it does happen, once in a life-time we hear of some weak, unbalanced man or woman doing some rash deed because of the temporary insanity of love; but in everyday life, men mourn for a time, and even if they carry the scar to their dying day, they will have good digestion, acquire the power to eat and sleep as of yore and in time find another object to tie their affections to, and go on, becoming good citizens and sober industrious members of society. So, let the world wag on in its usual way, now patting us on the back, anon thumping us on the head. Well for you and me, if we can always sense the fact that, after all, the one that gives pats and thumps is guided by an unseen hand, and each is for a wise purpose in God.

Part IX

As Aunt Sarah's health continued to wain during the whole summer and fall of 1860, Aseneth was persuaded to stay at the farm until the winter school was open, so that Willard had ample opportunities for studying the character of the girl he had at last resolved to seek for a wife. Such study could but serve to impress him with the innate nobility of the young girl. When with her, he felt a sense of peace and rest that had never been his since he had left his dear wife behind him. Indeed, the whole influence of Aseneth's character was one of unusual loving trust. The power he had felt in the love of his boyhood had been one of passion rather than peace. Now, he was quietly happy to sit down by this old fashioned Mormon girl and watch the supple fingers fashion garments for the little Mainwaring girls, or, with a copy of his magazine, read to her sympathetic ears the stories of all that was taking place in the Eastern States.

So the weeks came and went on the farm until fall had almost deepened into winter. As for the folks up at the city home, poor little Rhoda had found it almost more than she could endure to see the man she so deeply loved deliberately turn away from her and seek someone else.

"Oh Lou," she sobbed, when at last she poured all her troubles into her sister's loving ears, "I just hate that girl with her smooth ways. I just know she is a hypocrite. Talk about persuading her to stay down there to nurse Aunt Sarah! It is all a plot to catch Will."

"Now, Rhoda, don't go too far, for neither you nor I ever saw anything in 'Seneth like hypocrisy. She is as clear and straight up and down as you or I. I don't think you ought to hate her for loving the man you yourself think is so wonderful nice. That is not any crime. Land o'mercy, her having him needn't prevent you from having him too, so far as that goes."

Rhoda sat straight up. "Say, Lou, I never thought of that. Oh you don't know how I feel! I am sure I don't know what ails me. I am just fool enough to be willing to marry him if he wanted to go in second. But, you know," in her own honest way, "I would lots rather be first."

"Well I don't see anything wrong in thinking a good deal of a man. I think the wrong comes in our setting up our love before our religion. If our Father in heaven sees Willard is the one for you to have, He can bring it about in His own time and way. If I were you, I should ask Him to take the love out of your heart if it is not right, and if it is, to grant your desire in the future. That's what mother has always taught us is the way for us to do."

Impulsive little heart, "Oh, but I can't wait and wait for years maybe, you don't know what it is to feel as if the earth was a barren place without the man you love. I just can't bear it," and she broke out into a fresh shower of tears and she realized all "years" might mean to her.

"Well, dear, you can't help it as I see, unless you ask Willard to take pity on you and –"

"Lovina!" indignantly protested the sobbing girl, "you know I would die sooner than do anything like that."

The talk ended in some loving words of comfort and advice from Lovina; and, when she could, Lou went to her mother and told her the whole story. The two women, without betraying the girl's secret, even to father, contrived to arrange for a trip to some distant southern settlement; the mother going down to her sister's who had moved to Cedar City to live, and taking with her her daughter Rhoda. When Aunt Mary came back, we were surprised to find she had left Rhoda there to spend the whole winter. What lessons of patience and faith were learned by our little impulsive friend when absent from home and parents will transpire later in the course of this narrative.

To Willard, the city home seemed a trifle empty and lonely when his duty led him there, but he asked no one where Rhoda had gone or when she would return. He knew she would not thank him for any undue interest in her affairs, or he thought he knew it. He had conquered his feelings insomuch that the thought of Rhoda and her winsome eyes was only a sad one, not in any way bitter or regretful.

As the fall work had shifted from his shoulders, Willard began his work on a house for himself across the field from Aunt Sarah's. Early and late he toiled with as much vigor and a great deal more innocent gratification than he had worked at the tasks set him by his benefactor the Bishop.

"Aunt Sarah," he said one cold, stormy morning in the last of November, "when this storm clears off and I can get at my house once more, it will not take me more than three weeks to finish the whole. One week of outside work, and then I can bid defiance to wind or weather."

"Then I suppose you will be inviting us to a wedding dance to celebrate the joyful event," joked Aunt Sarah.

"Well, I want to," answered Will, looking into Aseneth's eyes with as direct and significant a glance as he could.

While at work that day Willard resolved to find out how Aseneth felt, and, let me be an honest historian, he felt little doubt or hesitancy as to the result. With all of his sensitiveness and good sense, he was yet a man and had all a man's traditionary faith in himself and his superior charms. I am sure I don't want to be led into using a sarcastic tone in speaking of my good friend Willard, but that particular state of mind in which we find him at this stage of life always excites my combativeness and my ridicule. A callow youth and an inordinately selfish man are alike subject to the disease I call the "enlargement of conceit." It is sometimes a dangerous affair, for I have known it to "strike in," creating more confusion of the whole organization than a dozen cases of "struck in" measels. For, unlike the measels, it can neither be purged out nor sweated out. If allowed to "settle," it will so engorge the bump of self esteem that years of experience have little effect in making a cure. I have seen a few women in my life who were skilled in eradicating this terrible complaint, but it generally happens that a poor woman who undertakes a chronic case finds at the end of her toils that her "esteem" has gone along with the remnants of the wretched man's "self esteem." So I always rejoice when I hear of a man who is impregnated with this disease finding some women, or, perchance, some fortunate circumstance which helps him to recover from his complaint ere time has made it chronic. I must say here, in justice to Willard, that his unlucky experience with Rhoda had, unmeant by the poor, innocent cause of it, a somewhat refreshing effect in showing him that he was neither so fascinating nor so smart as he had unconsciously supposed himself to be. A truce to moralizing, let us get on with the story.

That evening and for several evenings following, Willard sought to have a private interview with Aseneth. Either the girl herself or Aunt Sarah in her way prevented this design from being carried into effect.

When Sunday came, the young man determined to take matters into his own hands. So, he boldly invited Aseneth to go up to town with him, there to visit with her folks while he got his mail and did a few other necessary errands, adding that they could thus attend meeting in the tabernacle and have the privilege, perhaps, of hearing the President speak. Aseneth gave a quiet assent to his proposition, and at seven in the morning they rode out of the farm gate. They did not get away, however, without a parting shot from Aunt Sarah who desired them to have matters arranged about that forthcoming wedding before they returned. This failed to annoy Willard as it would have done at other times as he was glad to have the girl a little prepared, as it were. So away they drove, the cold, frosty air of early December tingling in their cheeks and making their general allowance of buffalo robes a genuine luxury.

For at least a half hour they rode in almost complete silence. Then Willard again resolved to take the law into his own hands and, albeit with much embarrassment, remarked, "Aunt Sarah has an odd way of telling people what to do."

"We can always excuse her, for she means no harm," answered the girl calmly.

"Especially when we want the same thing she does," laughed the young man.

The girl made no reply to his weak joke, and they rode again in silence. Then, with a visible effort, Willard said, "Well, I am not ashamed to know that Aunt Sarah's penetrating eyes have discovered my secret, and I thank her for her interest in my affairs."

Again no reply. So he went on, desperately, "Aseneth, will you mind if I tell you that I want Aunt Sarah's words to come true. I have wished that I might find favor in your sight for this long time. I am a poor, lone fellow without means or relatives, but I can work. And I have felt for years that I must have a home and family to help me to do my duty as an Elder in Israel."

The girl listened quietly without any words of reply.

"Now, ever since I became acquainted with you and your noble character, I have determined to win you as my wife," adding as an afterthought, "if I could."

Still no reply.

The man grew rather uncomfortable as this silence continued. "You are not offended with me, Aseneth, are you, for speaking so freely?"

"Offended, oh no." The voice was so quietly calm as if discussing an impersonal subject. "What should I be offended at?"

That staggered Willard, and he had no reply to the question. So they rode again in silence. After about ten minutes the girl turned her lovely, calm eyes on her companion and said, "And you want me to be your wife. I never really thought about such a thing before." And he knew she told the truth, for her tone was that of conviction. "You see, I thought you were in love with Rhoda." Then she had fathomed his carefully guarded secret and told him of it before he could confide it to her. This was getting to be rather warm work, even on such a cold day. But he had started in and he was not made of such stuff as cowards are, so he determined to tell her the whole truth. And he did, not sparing himself when talking to blame Rhoda. He was noble enough to take the blame upon himself when talking to another and indeed, if he had not been, I should never wanted to be his historian. The whole story, from the stolen kiss to the tossed slipper, and then he sank into a somewhat moody silence, waiting to hear what his companion would say to him.

"So, Brother Gibbs, you have been in love with two women, and now you fancy you are in love with another. For a young man, that's not so slow."

How horribly fickle he did seem, now that there was some one to paint the picture for him. What could ail him?

"You will not mind if I ask you some questions?"

"Of course not," answered Willard.

"Do you still love your wife in the east? As well as you ever did?"

"Yes I do," he answered passionately. "I would be a poltroon indeed were I afraid to acknowledge that."

"I should despise you were you to seek to deny it, Brother Gibbs. What would you do were she to join the Church and come to Utah?"

"Oh, you know what I should do, thank God with all the strength of my soul. I have talked with you about this, and you know that such a thing is the burden of my daily prayer."

"You must bear with me, for I want to know the position you take. Now, if your wife were to come here, say in the course of ten years, and find you married and settled down, what would you do?"

"You mean, would I want to get rid of my Utah wife to marry her?"

The girl's eyes opened wide with astonishment. "What do you mean? Get rid of the wife that was sealed to you for time and all eternity? How could you do that?"

"See here, Aseneth, you are tying me all up in your arguments. Suppose you just take this conversation in your own hands and let me listen. I will try to answer all your questions if you will not puzzle me too much." Certainly this was so unlike any wooing he had ever seen or even dreamed of that he was content to let the weaker vessel do the steering, for awhile at least.

"You must think me an odd girl, but, remember, you have asked me one of the most sacred questions ever asked on earth, and I was not expecting it, either. But I will confess, I have wondered what you would do if your wife were to come suddenly from the east and find you married. Do you believe in plurality of wives?"

"I am glad I can answer your question with a clear conscience that I do."

"But do you expect to go into that principle?"

"I don't hardly know. I can see it is virtually going into it to marry when I have a wife living. But I never thought I should be good enough to be able to live with two wives at once. It is not necessary for all men to go into, you know that, and if I never oppose it or talk against it I think I shall come out all right."

"Perhaps so, but you must remember that none of us will ever get any reward that we have not earned. It would be foolish for you or me to expect to go where those will go who learn far more than we do, pass through more than we do. Now, I don't think for one moment that a man will find polygamy an easy thing to live. And, if he fancies that the only lessons to be learned in it are those a woman learns, he will wake up to find his mistake. Of course a woman has seemingly the worst of the bargain, but that is because it teaches her to depend on God instead of her husband. Now, Brother Gibbs, I have never thought of marrying you, nor anyone else in particular, so far as that goes, but one thing I do know, and that is that I shall marry a man, if I can, who is not only willing but worthy to enter into the sacred bonds of plural marriage. Let us quit this subject for the present and leave it in the hands of the Lord."

Willard was very willing to accede to this proposal, but he had too many new and conflicting thoughts and emotions to talk much, so once again they fell into silence. Just as they were driving into the outer edge of town, Aseneth turned to her companion and said timidly, "Have you made this matter a subject of prayer?"

"No, not much," he was obliged to answer. He did not add that this constant turning to the Lord for guidance was at direct variance with his American traditions of manly independence.

The girl, conscious of his thoughts, ventured to say, "Shall we not do so? It seems to me to be a very solemn thing."

Willard rather savagely yet silently coincided with that last observation as this mode of courtship was not at all to his mind or taste. However, he contrived to make some indirect reply, and then they were at the house and he helped her to alight.

Verily, "Mormon" girls were a strange combination of humility and independence, he decided, and he was not sure that the combination was as disagreeable as one might think. One thing was sure, he was more determined than ever to get this quiet, placid girl for his wife if he could. Nor was his self esteem in so much danger of engorgement as it would have been if Aseneth had been other than she was. Altogether it certainly looked to an unprejudiced observer as if Providence had a hand in his life and labors.

On arrival at the house he learned that Aunt Mary had just returned from her trip to Cedar and that Rhoda had been left down there for the winter. He had a message from Aunt Sarah, who had sent up for Aunt Mary's youngest child, a little girl of about eight, to come and spend a week with them now that her mother was at Cedar.

Aunt Mary let the child go anyway, for she was wild with delight to think of spending a whole week at the farm. Hattie was a bright, nervous child, with a tongue of flame. Not so witty as Tommy, she was neither as cunning to say nothing to her own injury. She was a pet at home and was allowed to let her tongue rattle away at its own sweet will. Great was her delight when she found herself really in the carriage between Willard and Aseneth and en route to the farm.

They found Aunt Sarah prostrated. She had been taken in with a sudden spasm of cleanliness and had undertaken to give the whole place a thorough cleaning. Aseneth's ideas of neatness and hers were hardly the same, and she thought to administer a stern rebuke in the form of a house shining with cleanliness when the two travelers should return. Poor Aunt Sarah, she generally paid dearly for her "spurts," and now, indeed, she was unable to rise from her bed to say a word of greeting to her returned "travelers."

The next day she was a little better and had Hattie come in to visit with her. In the flood of Hattie's talk Aunt Sarah caught one word that arrested her attention.

"Did you say, Hattie, that your mamma was tired of living in the city home?"

"Oh, yes, you know since George died and now Rhoda has gone away, mamma wants to get away to some other place."

"Perhaps she wants to come down here?"

"Yes, I think she does, maybe. It is such a nice place down here, you know; and maybe papa will come down here more and more when the ward is fixed up."

"And then how nice for your mamma to be here and be the President of the Relief Society; wouldn't it be fine?"

"Yes, I guess mamma would like that. She is papa's first wife, you know."

"To be sure she is, and if she comes down here, she can boss us all down here. We need bossing, don't you think we do?" and the speaker laughed her unmirthful laugh.

"Yes, my mamma can do anything, for she is just the smartest woman that ever lived on this earth."

More of this kind of talk followed, and the child was quizzed, and the ideas were suggested to her, and her comments thereon were taken and carefully treasured up. Hattie spent several afternoons at the houses of the nearest neighbors, and her mind had been set agoing on the subject of her mother's coming down there to live. The prospect was very agreeable to the child, and she talked of nothing but her mother's probable removal.

Some of the neighboring sisters were free to say, in the hearing of the child, that they would be only too pleased if her mother was to come down and be the President of the Relief Society. The ward had never been organized as they were not in a suitable condition, being so scattered. Now, however, so many new families had moved down that there was talk of calling a bishop and organizing a Relief Society.

We will not follow Aunt Sarah in all that she did and said for the next month, for it was a time of great trial and temptation to her ambitious, somewhat unscrupulous nature.

On Christmas they all went up to the city home to spend the day. In the evening of that day Willard went over to the home of the Langs and asked Aseneth's mother if he might spend the evening there.

"Willard," she had asked to him that night when he had been talking to her, "if you want to see me and be my friend in very deed, you will gain the respect of my parents first. I could not marry anyone that they disapproved of."

Here was some more old fogy notions that he thought the light of the nineteenth century had driven into oblivion. The idea of courting the mother and father of the girl he wanted to marry! However, he found he had to learn that lesson as well as many others set before him by this "Mormon" girl.

That was a merry Christmas night, for the family joined in song, in corn popping and candy making with such earnestness that none remembered that they were thousands of miles from civilization and out in the deserts of the West.

"Aseneth," Willard whispered when he sat near the girl as she was shelling corn, "I am puzzled, I really don't know what to say or do to please you and make you like me."

"Don't you?" and she looked around and met his eyes full upon her; then, she colored in spite of herself and the blush on her pale cheek made her seem very charming. "Well, I am afraid if I tell you what to do, you will think it another of my odd notions and maybe laugh at me for it."

"Try me," and his breath on her cheek stirred even her calm pulses.

"Well, first you must please our Father in heaven, then you must please my dear father, then win my mother over to you, and after that you shall have a chance to persuade me to listen to you."

"You set me a hard task, I am afraid, but I shall not lose you for lack of trying to accomplish it. I am going to ask your father this very night if he will try and fall desperately in love with me."

"That's a good beginning," quietly laughed the girl.

Part X

The good merchant's wrath on hearing Willard's story was neither pleasant nor profitable.

"You come and ask me for my girl when I know nothing about you but your disreputable conduct towards us all in that miserable affair of the paper. I am ashamed of my daughter that she has so little sense of decency as to encourage you. You ask me for the most sacred privilege with as much assurance as you would if asking for a drink of water. No, sir, I will not give my consent to your having my Aseneth."

"You are mistaken, Brother Lang, if you think I do not appreciate the full importance of the privilege I have asked you to grant me. I should not wish to marry your daughter if I did not think her the best woman on earth and worthy of my devotion and love. I cannot see why you should hold a foolish and wicked lie so long in your belief and let it influence you against me. I told you at the time that it was a lie, and now I repeat it. I can do no more."

"No one asks you to do anything at all about it; but I guess there was some fire where there was so much smoke. I am not going to discuss the matter with you. I say, once and for all, I shan't give my consent for you to become my son-in-law. Good evening, sir."

And Willard found himself bowed out of the house and walked so hastily and angrily away that he forgot he had not told Aseneth the result of the interview or said good night.

He called for her next morning, however, and then told her all her father had said. The ride down to the farm was a frosty one that morning, and the girl seemed too cold to talk much. So Willard relapsed into silence after his story was told. Poor Willard was almost discouraged. It seemed there was some evil influence at work to hinder from securing any comfort or happiness in a home and family. At least it was very disheartening. He felt little interest in the new log house and spent the next two or three days in reading and something that looked very much like sulky silence.

Lying awake one night and pondering on the circumstances which had led up to this state of affairs, a remark made by Aseneth drifted idly into his mind. Had he made the matter a subject of prayer, she had asked him? Then came the remembrance of his own resolve at a former time to be more childlike in his faith and not trust so much in his own strength. He recalled the time when he had determined to ask God for a testimony on this very matter but he had failed to do so, his mind dwelling more on the girl than on the Lord or His purposes. He wondered in a half idle fashion if God really did take cognizance of such things as this. Then again his mind drifted away to something else, and he was again in the dark.

On New Year's day, the Bishop came down to spend the the day and told them he intended spending most of the winter with them. No one was more pleased to hear this than Willard. He resolved to see the Bishop alone and have a good talk with him. The day after New Year he invited the Bishop to go over to his little home and see what had been done in his absence. On the way over Willard opened his heart to his kind friend and showed him all the perplexities and difficulties he had so recently met.

"What shall I do? How shall I convince Brother Lang that I am an honest man, and how shall I get his consent to marry his daughter? For she says she will not have me without it, and I am discouraged. I reckon I am not worthy of a wife," with a mournful smile.

"Brother Willard, you ask me what you shall do and how you shall do. Let me ask you a question: have you asked the Lord anything about it?"

Willard looked blank, then colored clear up to his forehead.

"No, sir, I don't think I have specially mentioned the matter in my prayers. It seems rather strange to go to the Lord with every little thing. If He grants us the common blessings of life and then gives us the light of the gospel, it seems as if we ought to use our own common sense about our daily affairs and not bother the Lord for that which He has given us reason to get for ourselves."

"If that is the way you feel, why don't you get what you want yourself without coming to me for advice? The only value my advice would have would be because it was dictated by the good Spirit. You will have many lessons to learn if you try to live your life in your own strength. It is hard enough to live so as to gain an exaltation when you have all the help you can get from God; but I never heard of any way of pleasing God but by the Spirit of God."

The quietly spoken rebuke, the firm tone, made Willard feel ashamed and humble. He said nothing for some minutes then asked, "Do you think God interferes in the daily affairs of life? I have always thought that things go on without much interference from heavenly assistance, except where there is some special need of outside aid."

"Our Father deals with us on something the same principle as we deal with our children; if we seek the aid and counsel of our parents, they are always pleased and proud to grant it. All laws are in His hands, and we know comparatively nothing of the many laws and principles that govern

His actions. We know one or two of the ABC's of life, such as, if we put our fingers in the fire, they will burn. But the law by which God said to the fiery furnace, 'burn not the Hebrew children,' we know nothing about. It was a law, however, which is as simple as that of the combustion of the elements composing the fire, if we understood it. So on the same principle, there is a law of prayer and the answer to prayer. If God can control the flames, so can He hold the hearts of the children of men in His hands. You ask me what to do about gaining the consent of Brother Lang for your marriage with his daughter, I tell you to go and ask God to help you."

"And do you really think He will hear and answer my prayer on such a matter?"

"I know it. But there is another point connected with the principle of prayer. So many people think prayer is a sort of haphazard thing, when in reality it is as much a principle of order and law as anything else in the gospel. Saints, especially those who have received the keys of the holy Priesthood, should remember they possess great power with the heavens, and try to use that power wisely. Moroni tells us to be careful what we pray for, not to ask for that which is inexpedient for us to have. In other words, beware that we ask not to consume it on the lusts of the flesh. With the most of us, we do not ask for half that we should.

"I think the American air must be too free for the most of men, for it is generally counted as a weakness to pray for that which we can get without troubling God."

They were at the new house then, and the Bishop ended the conversation by remarking, "Our Savior is our guide in all these matters, and if we are ashamed of Him and His ways, He will be very apt to be ashamed of us in the day of our trial."

Willard, like many of the rest of us, was much more impressed and agreed with his friendly counselor more than he felt to acknowledge, so for the present he let the subject die. He resolved in his own mind to make the whole principle a matter for study and reflection. It is enough to say here that he more or less faithfully carried out his resolve and the future events of his life were one constant proof of the Bishop's words.

He was too proud to trouble either Aseneth or her father with his feelings, and so they two, Willard and Aseneth, were somewhat cool and reserved in their behavior for the next few weeks. Willard had so far overcome his proud nature as to pray in set and earnest words twice a day for the heart of Brother Lang to be softened towards him. And the course of three months he received a singular answer to his prayer.

One afternoon in early March the Bishop told him he had a message from President Young for him; it was a request for him to come up to his office as soon as he could. In great wonderment of mind as to what this might mean, Willard went at once to comply with the request.

On reaching the city he found quite a crowd of people in the office waiting for a chance to see the President. So he sat down and patiently waited his turn. When at last the clerk came and asked him his name and his business, he was weary and had lost whatever curiosity he might at first have felt. The first look into the kindly eyes of the President dispelled his annoyance, and he shook the hand of Brother Brigham for the first time in his life with a feeling of pleasure and gratitude.

"So you are the young man who left wife, home and child in Virginia to come to Zion? I am glad to meet you, Brother Gibbs. Sit down and tell me about yourself."

It seemed easy to tell all the sad and painful details of his entering the Church to this good man, for there was a warmth of sympathy that drew his story from him without an effort. When the tale was finished, the President said, "Well, Brother Gibbs, you have had quite an experience. How long have you been here?"

"Nearly 2 years."

"And have you got you a home and a wife yet?"

"No sir. I think I am rather unlucky at that sort of thing. I have a good log house down near Bishop Mainwaring's farm, but I can find no one foolish enough to marry me."

The note of pain in the speaker's voice was plainly apparent to the sharp ears of the man who read the hearts of his fellow men at a glance. He made no answering comment but said, "Brother Gibbs, we want you to take a mission to England for a couple of years. But I feel as if I should like to see you have a family before you leave here. Have none of our comely girls found a warm spot in your heart?"

Willard turned his hat around and around. Theretofore he had felt no embarrassment in speaking; but now, he knew not what to say. If he said anything, he would betray his own pride and lack and faith which he now felt had been the real barrier between him and Aseneth as well as the unfortunate feud between Brother Lang and himself. He had all a proud, spirited man's horror at talebearing. And yet he could not but answer this direct question. After a somewhat lengthy pause, he answered, "Yes, sir, there is a girl that I, that she, that we, that is –"

The President broke into an irresistible smile, and Willard laughed at his own embarrassment and awkwardness.

A few skillful, direct questions brought the whole thing out; and after listening in silence to Willard's hurried explanations, Brother Young answered, "You come up here at ten o'clock tomorrow and I will have Brother Lang up here and we will talk the matter over. For the present, then, we will say good afternoon."

Willard's sleep was filled with vague, uneasy dreams that night, and it was with a very humble, childlike spirit that he bowed before his Maker the next morning, for he knew he was weak wherein he had for years thought himself strong, and he was full of a desire to become so meek that God would listen to his prayers and give his wisdom to know what to pray for. He was pale with the intensity of his feelings, and his knees felt suspiciously like trembling as he opened the outer office door and saw Brother Lang sitting near the door.

"Now, brethren," said the President after they were alone, "we will talk over this matter in the spirit of Saints. Brother Gibbs, we will listen to your explanation in regard to your associations with Arthur Willis. Now, don't be afraid to tell just what happened."

So encouraged, Willard told his part of the affair, and then, feeling a spirit of confession come over him, he acknowledged his fault – so he termed it – in seeking to gain a good girl's heart and hand without first asking God to be his guide and hourly counselor. He frankly confessed to Brother Lang that he was, no doubt, too proud and self-sufficient.

"You have reached one of the home truths of our religion, Brother Gibbs," remarked President Young when his recital was ended, "to keep your heart humble before God and to seek your brethren in the spirit of love and good fellowship is one of the keys to the door of happiness here and hereafter. You showed to Brother Lang, from your own confession, a spirit of unbending pride and expected to receive his consent for your marriage to his daughter without one moment's consideration of all the bitterness and sorrow your thoughtless but unfortunate actions had caused him. Our daughters, the sweet pure souls of the daughters of Zion, are our pride and our joy, and we fathers part with them with reluctance and misgivings. And, Brother Gibbs, I am but repeating Brother Lang's sentiments and my own when I say we would prefer men who have been tried and proven in this gospel and in life as husbands for their affections. I know Bro. Lang's Aseneth, and she is a good, dutiful girl, a precious prize to the man who is fortunate enough to get her. You must understand that fact. Also that you are not as yet fully proven. On the other hand, Brother Lang, this young man was not particularly to blame in that paper affair, and as soon as he learned the character of the apostate, he shunned him. He has done well since then and bears a good name in his ward.

Bishop Mainwaring speaks very highly of him and told me but last week that he has enough confidence in him to give him one of his own daughters if he had asked for one."

Willard's unruly heart still had recollection enough to throb strangely at this high compliment paid him.

"Come, now, Brother Lang, what do you say?" went on the President. "Let us arrange this matter. Brother Gibbs tells me Aseneth is quite willing to have him if you will give your consent. The mother is doubtless willing also. We want Brother Gibbs to start on a mission to England, but if he gets married, we will give him three months to settle his wife in her new home and arrange his affairs to leave."

After some further conversation, Brother Lang gave his consent and the two men left the office together. I would not pretend to say that Brother Lang felt all his prejudices removed, for he was a man of obstinate ideas, but he enjoyed sufficient of the Spirit of the Lord to see that the thing was right and he tried to put aside his bitterness and treat the young man with as much friendliness as he could.

It was arranged before leaving the office that Willard and Aseneth were to be at the Endowment House on the fast day of next month, April, and get back at once to their new home to prepare for his mission.

Willard's horse made excellent time to the farm that evening, and he reached home just as the big moon peeped over the hill.

The front room was empty, and sounds from the front bedroom indicated that Aunt Sarah was brooding her little ones into their snug nests. He passed through the front room, and as he stepped into the kitchen, the dim light of the tallow candle showed Aseneth standing by the sink washing up the milk things. He walked up quietly, and putting both arms closely around her, he bent his head down, and kissed her startled eyes and lips and whispered, "I am going on a mission, my dear."

She wiped her hands on her apron and turned herself around in his arms as she asked with almost a gasp, "When?"

"Do you really want to know when?" he could not refrain from teasing, he was so happy. "Do you really care?"

Her eyes asked and answered for her.

"Well, then, I am going to England, after – after," and he drew her closer yet, "after you and I are married," his lips closed to her cheek, "and settled in our new home."

The love and intense feeling of his words and manner had beguiled her into forgetfulness of her vow of obedience to parental authority, so now with the reminder of his words she put his arms away and said faintly, "I don't think you realize what you are saying."

"Oh, yes I do, though. But one thing I do not know," his quick temper rising, "and that is whether you care one bit for me or not. I shall not say another word about myself or my plans until I know something more about you. I do believe you are incapable of love such as I feel."

He sat down by the kitchen table, and, dropping his head in his hands, reflected on the singularity of womankind in general, and the oddity of this particular girl.

Part XI

Aseneth stood for a moment near the sink, slowly drawing down her turned up sleeves, and looked with quivering lips at the man whose arms had so closely clasped her that she could still feel their presence. Another moment of indecision, then slowly she stepped to his side and, sinking down to her knees, she laid a timid hand on his knee.

"Willard," she murmured, "why are you so hasty? See me, dear, I am here, and if I am not willing to disobey my parents, it is not because I do not – love you."

He drew her up to him and murmured.

"It is the very first time you have ever owned to loving me, Aseneth, and I have told you my feelings so many times that I felt aggrieved. Now in order to make your restitution complete, my girl, you must kiss me of your own free will and accord; then I will tell you of the good things which have befallen us and all about your father's giving his consent."

"Has father given his consent?" And she sprang up with eager delight.

"Yes, my dear," drawing her back to him, "you might as well remain here, for you see I have the right now to hold you," and he playfully pinched her ear.

That was a short yet long hour they spent in happy converse; the poor candle grew so long as to wick so short as to tallow that it set up at last a dim sputtering remonstrance which for the nonce was totally unheeded by Aseneth's careful fingers.

It was certainly near midnight when the two arose and said good night. As Aseneth looked up into his darkly beaming brown eyes, she whispered under her breath, "Thank God!"

"What's that?"

She hesitated, and then repeated her exclamation of gratitude. "Willard it is not always those who can show their feelings and act them out who feel the deepest. My way may not be as gushing as some, but I can be faithful and will love you I know forever and forever."

The words seemed drawn from her usually reserved, silent lips by the excitement of the moment. But ah, faithful true heart, how truly dids't thou prophesy that night! Faithful, fond and true, even in these latter years of persecution and gloom, faithful even unto death and prison bars.

Willard vaguely realized that he had won a prize of unusual worth even among the fair and worthy daughters of blest Utah.

I will not linger over the hasty preparations for the wedding: the few articles of underwear, the two new dresses, the "pillow slips" and coarse sheets which Aseneth's slow but careful fingers furnished and finished. The Mainwarings made haste to piece and quilt two good, serviceable bed quilts to aid in the new house furnishing, Aseneth's mother made up twelve yards of rag carpeting, the tearing, sewing, coloring and weaving all being done by her own hands.

Aunt Sarah undertook to make the white swiss wedding dress and to cook the wedding supper.

During those days of preparation Willard worked from daylight till long after dark, making and getting such simple furniture as was necessary for the ordinary wants of their home.

The day before the wedding Brother Lang came down and overwhelmed both Willard and Aseneth with the present of a good carpet loom he had got on a trade. This was a very valuable present, for it would mean a comfortable living with a chance to save something, perhaps, while Willard was on his mission. The good merchant was pleased in his daughter's happiness and gratitude and pretty successfully concealed the lingering traces of his dislike to his future son-in-law.

On the morning of the 2nd of April, 1861, the party from the farm drove up to the city and went straight to the Endowment House.

After giving in their names to the clerk, President Heber C. Kimball came to the table and shaking hands with them all he put his hand on Willard's shoulder and said, "God bless you, Brother Gibbs, and preserve you from danger by flood and by fire, by shot and by shell. Your labors shall be many, your reward shall be sure. You shall drag your sheep from the bowels of hell and return to the fold with it close to your heart. Go in peace and return in safety. Don't leave your heart here behind you, but put Sister Aseneth in the hands of God. As soon as you leave Great Salt Lake City, leave every care, every burden, every thought behind you but the burden of your mission. God will not accept of half-hearted labors. Be single hearted and you shall receive the blessings."

Then they were married and the whole Mainwaring and Lang families drove at once back to the farm where Aunt Sarah was awaiting them, her table, as the good Bishop said in his blessing, "spread with the rich bounties of life."

Of course there was much laughter and jest, and Willard was obliged to keep a steady head and a quick tongue to parry off the many shafts of good natured railery and wit leveled at his and Aseneth's heads.

Rhoda had not returned from the south, and in his heart Willard was glad she had not. It was better so.

After the clatter of dishes had subsided and everybody was for the moment silent, sitting still at the table loth to rise from the place where all had so enjoyed themselves, the Bishop spoke up, and looking down at the young couple opposite him remarked: "Brother Willard, there are a few things I wish to say to you. You have now taken upon yourself the solemn obligations of a family. And let me say to you that the responsibility of your own life and that of your wife or wives as well as your children rests mainly upon you. You are the head. See to it that you lead in the right direction. Don't worry about what your wives or children may or may not do. Do your own duty fully, faithfully; guide, counsel, walk in the line of your duty, and you can leave the rest with God. Never sacrifice principle to please any woman, or you may find you have added your soul's salvation to the sacrifice and lost it. You are the stronger vessel, and must needs bear the heavier burdens. Be kind and loving always to your family, but do not be weak and indulgent. God expects strength and obedience to Him from you, and gentleness and obedience to you from your wife. Her love and obedience are only promised to you on conditions of your obedience to the gospel. This I want to impress upon all my sons: if they are faithful and true to their covenants, their wives can never get away from them in all eternity; but if they violate those sacred obligations they have made, they will not only be punished themselves, but their wives will be taken from them and given to a worthier man."

"That's all very well, pa," spoke up sharp tongued Aunt Fanny, "but there's such a thing as a man getting a deceitful hussy for a wife, and she can make lots of trouble and misery."

The Bishop looked across at his wife but did not answer for a moment. Then, "You are right, Fanny; but if a husband does his duty and is a man, his wives will sooner or later learn to respect his wishes and to love each other. Each soul must win its own salvation, but women are much better, naturally, than men. I have a great admiration for the sisters."

Then the talk drifted to other subjects and the rest of the evening was spent in laughter and chat, frolic and fun.

Willard had slipped away to the new house and had lighted a fire in the fireplace, for the evening was cool; as he stood looking around the room, the homemade bed in one corner, the big carpet loom in the opposite one, the floor carpeted half way with the bright new carpet, the deal table and two rush-bottomed chairs, the flashing fire sending its cheer over hearth and walls, the small array of tinware on the one shelf sending back into the blaze an answering twinkle of light, he lifted up his heart to God in a swift, silent prayer of gratitude and longing to remember the counsels of President Young and his kind friend, the Bishop. How simply yet effectually God had answered his prayers! He was too happy and grateful tonight to allow one skeptical doubt as to its being a coincidence. That might intrude later, but he had started in the right path to reach peace and a reliance upon a higher power, and it was ordained that he should learn the lesson fully and well.

An hour after he brought his bride with him. Going up the mantle piece Aseneth took something from it, and returning to Willard she put a small package in his hand.

"This was sent by Rhoda to us as a present. I have not opened it. Aunt Mary gave it to me today."

Willard untied the string and found a prettily worked needle book full of bright, new needles and daintily made, round pin cushion, each worked with a small flower, the pin cushion filled with bright-headed pins. The pins and needles were in themselves no small gift in those days, and the paper which fell out with the words,

> "With love, from your friend
> Rhoda"

filled Aseneth's heart with gratitude and her eyes with tears.

"Here, Aseneth, they are for you," said Willard.

"No, dear, she meant them for you to carry in your pocket while you are on your mission. Take them; indeed it will give me real pleasure to have you take them."

Willard looked down, deep into the tender, shining eyes, and asked himself if it were possible this girl meant what she said.

"Why, my girl, I should think you would be jealous."

"I hope God will keep me from ever being jealous," she answered in a low, earnest tone. "If you love me, surely I ought to be content."

That was a strange doctrine to the young man, but he refused to accept her offer.

"No, I shall not take them. You might feel badly about it after I am gone."

"Indeed I shall not, then. Please oblige me, dear."

"Well, if you are going to feel so badly about it, I will take the pin cushion, for it will be very handy. But the needle book you must certainly keep, for it would be useless to me, and certainly was not meant for me, either. Perhaps Miss Rhoda would be offended for me to take either. She does not have a very good opinion of me."

Then their talk drifted to the day just passed and to the future spread out before them, and after some whispered words of love and tenderness, they two knelt down by the high piled straw bed and dedicated their new home, their happiness and their lives to God and His kingdom.

Part XII

Rhoda Mainwaring came home from her protracted visit to the south just one month to the day after Willard had left the city. I cannot say that she did not keep the date of this departure sadly in her memory, but she was a healthy, sound-minded girl, and during her visit had learned many useful lessons. Never did she love her mother so well, never did she listen with such loving reverence to the kind words of counsel given her by her father at the evening prayer time. Her home seemed the sweetest place on earth and she entered into all the small home plans with a strong interest and pleasure.

She was too pretty and winsome to escape having plenty of that material to practice her cute ways upon, called in western dialect, "beaus," but some way they all remained "beaus," none became lovers. She would feel attracted to one for weeks at a time and under the influence of that attraction I am afraid she gave the youth strong encouragement to become loverlike. Whenever he accepted her preferences, however, as a hint for such conduct she would fly about like a windswept weathercock and begin to actually despise the "very ground he walked upon." I was often reminded of the very old comparison about the moths and candle at this period of Rhoda's life, and it did seem so strange that the lads themselves could not see how it would inevitably turn out.

Sometimes, indeed, a swain would prove rather "hard-headed," and then it was amusing to watch "my lady," for she seemed possessed of a spirit of perverse attraction to such a youth, and so bright, so winning, so variable was she in all her pretty moods that, sooner or later, the unlucky swain surrendered at indiscretion, and very soon thereafter joined the singed-wing gentry that marked her comet-like flight through the festivities of the time.

I am not prepared to defend Rhoda's conduct in these matters, indeed, she earned a very hard name from the "Singed-wing Corps," as Moroni derisively dubbed them, that of a "coquette." Perhaps she deserved it. One by one, however, they came, were seen and no matter how obdurate fell before the sweet eyes of the laughing girl.

There was one thing about her which softened my judgment of her conduct, and one other thing which raised her infinitely in my old fashioned mind. I knew well that the girl's heart was hungry and empty. She had struggled honestly to drive out the unwelcome image love had set up in her white soul, for she really believed her devotion to Willard was ill-placed, scorned and unwelcome; for this cause she eagerly sought to find a new object on which to pour the affection of her heart. It seemed to be neither her fault nor the fault of her many admirers that she was each time disappointed. I sometimes feared, though, that impulse might lead her to accept a transient attraction as a permanent affection and thus wreck her life. This was in God's hands.

The cause which so deepened my respect for the girl was a firm refusal to accept any attentions from married men. I knew men foolish enough to seek her society on the same footing as the young men took, but Rhoda openly refused to even come down into the parlor if they came "a-wooing."

"No," she told one flirting father, "if you want to come and see me, bring both of your wives with you. I don't intend to marry a married man, so you will do no good coming to see me. If I ever should break my resolution, be sure of one thing, I shall not walk over another woman's heart to my happiness. So if I want to marry you or any other married man, I shall do so without one hour's 'sparking.' The man who 'sparks' me and leaves other wives sorrowing at home while he does so would 'spark' other women after he got me and leave me at home to suffer as I had made others to suffer. No, sir, I don't care to have you come to see me, unless, indeed, you bring your whole family with you."

When she told me of this brave little rebuke which she administered to a gay married man, I knew my Rhoda was firmly intrenched behind the bulwark of principle, and I could leave her to God and her destiny without any fears.

Thus passed two years of the time which Willard spent on his mission.

Aseneth was a happy girl, and when, about eight months after Willard left, she became the mother of a little girl with dark curls all over the tiny head, she was so full of deep content that she hardly knew how to express her gratitude to God.

When the news reached her husband, he wrote:

Dearest wife:

Am I again a father to a child which mine eyes have never beheld? Two women have brought into this world spirits from God, clothed upon with part of my very being. I am the father of a son and a daughter, and still unblessed as yet with a single look into their little faces, a single kiss from the crumpled, rose-leaf cheeks. Ah, well, God is very merciful, very good! You must kiss my little daughter (how the name thrills my heart!) Morning and evening for her absent father.

I am trying, and I believe succeeding fairly well, in carrying out President Kimball's advice. Not often does my heart turn longingly to home, Zion, wife, but now the sweet addition of child is added, these few hours following the receipt of your letter have turned my heart homeward, and I don't think God is displeased with me for the tears of love, gratitude and joy which you see have already blurred much of this letter.

Always so unselfish, my good wife, your suggestion to call our baby after my lost Hortense filled me with a double sense of painful pleasure. You knew it would do so, did you not? I say, yes, a thousand times, Yes. I wish you would have taken this matter in your own hand and had her blest by the Bishop on the eighth day as is the custom in the Church. But never mind, I will take her in my arms when I come home and give her a father's blessing that I feel will go with her clear into eternity.

The letter contained many loving injunctions to the patient little wife in Utah and was read over many times in whispers to Mistress Hortense as she lay in pink helplessness near her mother's rocking chair.

"Any letters from Willard?" queried Lovina and Rhoda one day as they stood in the door, being down to Aunt Sarah's on a visit.

"Yes," answered Aseneth willingly, "but it's only a short one this time." She did not mention its extra sweetness, nor would she read it as she did sometimes his long, interesting descriptions of travel. Her fine sense of tact kept her silent while Rhoda was present.

"What does he have to say about our princess?" persisted Lou, who had lifted the pretty bundle from the homely home-made crib and was making the baby's eyes blink with the explosive kisses which she showered upon face and neck.

"Oh, he is pleased at my wanting to name her Hortense," answered Aseneth.

"Aseneth Lang– Gibbs!" with a tiny catch in Rhoda's voice at the last name, "you weren't generous enough to propose naming her after that woman?"

"Why not?" replied Aseneth calmly.

The question staggered Rhoda, for surely why should she have anything to say or think about a thing so manifestly none of her business. "Well!" she ejaculated, "you are certainly the oddest girl I ever saw."

"It shouldn't be odd to be as unselfish to others as you would like them to be to you," said Aseneth as she took the baby.

In some way the quiet words, the tiny bobbing head with dark curls so like the father's, the intense love shown by the mother in her quick caress, set Rhoda's mind off in a new channel of thought. What is love? What its best expression and what relation does it bear to life?

These questions were not formulated and reasoned out in the girl's mind, but a new train of thought, a new way of thinking about these matters sprang into being on the moment. Aseneth was, of course, utterly unconscious of the thoughts she had awakened by her simple, earnest words, and chatted idly with Lovina about Aunt Sarah's last baby and the shortening of baby Hortense.

"Aseneth is a splendid, good girl, isn't she?" said Rhoda as the two girls went back to Aunt Sarah's.

"She is that; I only wish we could be more like her."

"We can be, I guess, if we try. Mother always says we can be anything we want to be."

Lovina was thinking of her marriage to a young man from Farmington and wondering if she could be as good and unselfish in all her wifely acts. Rhoda's thoughts were very busy. She loved Aseneth's baby girl with a strange intentness that warned her how futile had been her efforts to forget the father. She had even successfully concealed her feelings, however, beneath of mask of light, laughing railery. Aseneth she could love, she knew, as a sister, for no one could resist the gentle, young wife; but how Aseneth could forgive the haughty, Gentile wife who had cast her husband aside from pride and intolerance, this was inexplicable to Rhoda. And to name her own baby after the woman, thus calling the hated image up to her husband's eyes every time she was mentioned! Certainly Rhoda could not comprehend it.

After, in the quiet of the night, in thinking the matter over, a sudden new vision of the wife in the East, alone, deserted, proud and loving, suffering both from her own doings and the notions of her adored husband, all this came to Rhoda's impulsive imaginative heart, called up by Aseneth's noble words, and she began dimly to see the wide, sweet path which Aseneth walked in, the path of unselfish love, find its chief joy in making the loved ones happy. Was that true love? She questioned. It was true love, and true Mormonism; and Rhoda had just begun to learn the lesson spread out on silent page of night reaching clear to the end of the Lamb's Book of Life.

In the winter of 1863, the following letter to Willard was forwarded by Aseneth to him in England:

Dear Friend Willard:

I write this last message before I join in this terrible war. I have endured the strain so long I am almost crazy. Mother writes me daily, urging, begging, commanding me to join the southern forces and 'stand up for the principle of right and justice.' While you know my own sympathies are all northern. My long association with my uncles in Philadelphia and the clear duty I owe to my native country drive me to accept a position in the northern army. I have hesitated between the two hell stools long enough. You may add in your own mind the rest of the adage. Well, maybe I shall fail; but even death would be a welcome release from the sufferings I have endured the last two years. Another element of uncertainty and half-misery has been added to my mind through those books you sent me. Willard, I am afraid they contain truth. The aims and ambitions of my life have fallen away from me even as a cloak that is threadbare and rotten; and I know instinctively that I am not morally brave enough to face all that you did for the truth of the Almighty. This haunts me nightly, while the face of war and the old familiar cries of 'honor' and 'country' grin and howl at me every hour of the day. To finish, I have enlisted in the Twenty-seventh Regiment of Pennsylvania Volunteers which goes at once to the seat of war in the Shanandoah Valley. We shall be under General Hooker and hope to succeed in driving Lee from his strong-hold in Fredricksburg.

I must tell you that poor Hortense is fairly wild. From her letters to me she is about as badly fixed as I am. She is all northern in her sympathies and being one who speaks her convictions freely, she and mother are daily fighting the country's battles over their work tables. Mother threatens dreadful calamities, and the poor girl would gladly leave if she possibly could. The child is her sole comfort and hourly torment, for mother constantly swears she will abduct the little fellow unless Hortense stays with her and helps the southern cause. I sent Hortense the little volume called

'Spencer's Letters,' but she has never acknowledged receiving it. If you possibly can do so, go down and see Hortense when you return from your mission, for some way I feel you could do her some good. Get her away from that hell hole if you can, for our old home is in the thick of the fight.

      Should you never hear from me again, always remember me as

                Your true friend,
                    Oscar"

This letter Willard sent to the Presidency in Utah and asked for counsel in the matter. Just a week before his release came, in September, 1863, he received answer, counseling him to go down into Virginia, if he could get there, and bring his wife and child back with him. A letter to Utah's delegate, Dr. J. M. Bernhisel, was enclosed, which would be of assistance in getting passports.

In the same mail was a letter from his staunch friend Bishop Mainwaring with an order on the P.E. Agent in New York City for $175.00, the letter telling Willard he had read his letter to President Young and he knew he would need some means to accomplish the desired object. The worthy Bishop concluded with a few simple words, reminding Willard of his two years' faithful labors in the writer's interests and that they were not forgotten.

Willard was so overjoyed he scarcely knew how to behave himself, but went out into the dirty streets of Liverpool and walked miles over the uneven pavement to cool down his enthusiasm, his mind constantly recurring to the popular refrain of the American war song "Glory, Glory, Hallelujah."

Part XIII

Nothing has been said of the many experiences endured and enjoyed by Willard during his two and a half years mission to England. My time and space will not allow the recital. But let me here say that he had more singular manifestations, realized more of the wonderful power held within the confines of this gospel than had ever entered his mind to dimly conceive. Miracles in the healing of the sick and especially of one born dumb, dreams of warning and of comfort, testimonies of the power of God, answers speedy and sure to fervent prayer, all these experiences he shared in common and which, when he had sufficiently humbled himself, he did learn, and that was to conquer the suddenness of his anger, the unruly heat of his tongue when annoyed. He felt his whole future earthly happiness depended on the lessons of self control gained by him under the peculiar mellowing influences of his English mission. Well for him that he did as he did, for no man can expect successfully to stand as head and guide of a family, especially a plural family, unless he stands as master over his own heart and his own tongue. Willard's fellow missionaries, the poor, often ignorant people with whom he associated, and the jeers and scoffs of those opposed to his belief were excellent material for his purpose, I am proud to say, he came out so nearly conqueror that his course was onward and upward from the very day he first set foot on English soil.

So now, in June of the year 1863, we find him landed in America and at once hurrying to the address of the emigration agent in New York.

Learning of the big battle being fought at Gettysburg and of the tremendous loss of life, his heart sank within him in some unaccountable way. He was told that it was Hooker's – now Meade's command, and that the Twenty-seventh Pennsylvania Volunteers were in the active line of battle and informed how useless it would be to try and get into the lines of the regular army.

This was a severe disappointment, for he was determined to see Oscar if possible and induce him to go with him to Utah.

He set out at once for Washington to get his passports and then on to Marysvale.

He found a warm friend in genial Doctor Bernhisel and through his influence obtained a permit for a passport from a prominent southerner who was well known to the doctor. Two weeks were unavoidably spent in getting the necessary papers, and Willard was warned that his undertaking was extremely dangerous.

The valuable lessons of reliance on a higher power than his own will or intelligence which he had learned in England made him brave with the bravery of a perfect faith.

His passports described him as a minister of the gospel in search of a southern wife; it was deemed advisable for him to wear clothes suitable to the description given of his character. Setting out from Washington on horseback, he had little trouble the first day.

Marysvale was a small village in upper Virginia set in a semicircle of hills not over ten miles from Warrenton on the east side of the Blue Ridge mountains. He was obliged to go down the Potomac as far as Aquia Creek at which point there was a southern battery, the fortification running up and down the Potomac for perhaps twenty miles.

He knew his life here must be in the hands of Providence, but he did not fear. Luckily for him his accent had the true Virginian twang, and he hoped to pass the provost guards with little trouble.

It required some money, much influence, and a good deal of faith to procure a passage down the river in a small Federal frigate which was intended to carry stores down to Fortress Monroe. He was warned that they were liable to have some engagement, but his anxiety and faith were much stronger than his fear or his doubts. So, having agreed that they would put him off on a small landing not far from Aquia Creek, he went aboard and the vessel was soon sailing smoothly down the Potomac.

His landing, of course, would have to be effected in the night and he would have to trust to "luck," the captain said, to get from there over to Warrenton or Marysvale. Willard's mind was about equally divided between the intense feeling of uneasiness about the fate of those he had come to seek and joy to find himself at last on the way for his old home.

That night was a cloudy yet sultry night in the southern summer latitude, the new moon seldom showing herself, and without incident to Willard, who lay on the tarry deck with his coat rolled up for a pillow, looking into the quiet, cloudy sky above him and wondering how his dear ones in Utah were as well as thinking anxiously of the fate of Hortense and his boy.

It was past midnight, nearly one o'clock in the morning when he was put off at the landing only a few miles below or above Aquia Creek.

He knew the road well, indeed, all the country laying between Aquia and Warrenton was familiar to him in his youth; and he did not forget how to find his way through the brush up to him up to a point where there used to be a cluster of houses just below the hill which overlooked the juncture of Aquia and the Potomac.

After he had stumbled along for about half an hour he heard a distant shot in the direction of the Aquia landing.

"The Yankee boat has been discovered," was his instant thought, as he saw the gleam of young moonlight.

He saw the shot and shell from ship and battery. Even as it flashed through his mind there was an answering volley and then shot and shell from ship and battery asked and answered various questions as to life and liberty.

Willard ran along the narrow path, and, just as a loud boom and a peculiar whizz announced the coming of a shell from the river boat, he stumbled over a narrow but deep chasm and lay partially in the rut, quite faint with the pain in a broken or sprained ankle. After a while, he raised himself slowly, and getting onto his feet with much difficulty, he found he was all but unable to get along.

The sprain was not severe, but it made traveling very uncertain and painful. The firing continued, and once he saw whizzing over his head an ugly shell, its fuse still twirling as it cut its way deliberately through the air.

His progress was very slow and after a while the shots and firing grew less and at last ceased. He knew he was near a human habitation, for as he now and then emerged from the thick brush into an open space, he caught sight of a light in some distant cabin.

Steering his way as best he could in the uncertain light, he emerged into the open space where the cabin stood and sat down on the ground to rest his aching limb and to discover, if possible, who and what the inhabitants of the place were.

It was nearly daylight now, and he saw from the dim light already kissing the lips of the uplifting eastern hills that it was certainly past four o'clock so that he had been two or three hours on the way from "Jones' Landing." How slowly he had traveled, for there at his back rose the hill on which the Aquia fortifications kept watch of the river. He could barely discern the outline of the works in the dim morning light. The hut still had the light shining from its window and the circular clearing in which it stood, surrounded by the forest of brush and small trees, proved that it was the habitation of some mountaineer or perhaps a guard's temporary dwelling.

Willard sat in the shadow of a tree across the clearing, and even as he turned his attention once more to the cabin, a man came out, his tall form outlined by the bright light behind him. He was dressed in the simple shirt and trousers of a mountaineer, a rough, furry cap surmounting his shock of long, unkempt hair. Willard had no way of knowing how he might be received by such a man and considered it wise to wait and watch for a few moments.

The man looked out at the slow rising dawn, and then, stepping out a few yards, he began evidently searching for something or things. He seemed to be successful, and Willard vaguely wondered what it could be, for the man gathered quite an armful of things and placed them together in a small pile; then, going into the house, he brought out a box, probably a cracker box so thought Willard who saw the box outlined by the light as the man passed through the doorway.

Gathering up the things he had piled up, he placed them in the box, and then, taking it into the house, Willard heard pounding which proved a lid was being fastened over the box. Coming out with the box under his arm, the man walked across the clearing to a spot not four rods from where Willard lay concealed and began digging.

"A grave?" asked Willard of his own strangely beating heart. Certainly yes. For the fast spreading light showed him that the hole was being shaped like a grave, and if more proof were were needed, it showed in the bloody condition of the man's hands.

Willard scarcely dared breathe. He had no idea of the nature of the tragedy evidently just enacted, but he had sense enough to wait until he knew more before betraying his presence to the man.

Once buried, the man spaded up the earth in the shape of a grave, which showed Willard that there was no desire for concealment, whatever the cause of all this. Then going to the cabin once more the man soon returned with a board, digging away the earth in order to set up the board, having evidently forgotten to do so in the first place. Taking a piece of charcoal, he carefully wrote something on the board, and then placing it properly again settled the clods in a rounded form, and with a low sigh, he picked up his spade and went back into the cabin.

Impelled by something stronger than mere curiosity, Willard crawled around, keeping in the edge of the brush forest, until he was near the small grave.

Straining his head carefully around the tree near which he crouched he read in the uncertain dawn in big printed letters the one word, "Harold."

He must have swooned, for he remembered nothing for some time until he felt a sudden severe twinge in his ankle, and he came to himself as the sun arose over the hilltops.

He remembered then that he was weak, faint and weary, and in a moment the black letters on the head board of the small grave close to him seemed to burn themselves into his brain.

He knew he must get around the path and thus approach the house lest he should create suspicion in the mind of the owner of the cabin.

With pain and difficulty he made his way slowly and carefully around to the path which was plainly shown in the daylight and approached the cabin as carelessly and indifferently as he could.

The moment he appeared in sight the old man was at the open door and watched his approach with keen if not suspicious eyes.

"Can I get something to eat here?" queried Willard as he neared the cabin.

"What's the matter with your ankle?" asked the old man.

Without telling too much Willard gave a brief outline of his trip from Washington and its object. No one, not even this suspicious mountaineer, had a moment's doubt about the truthfulness of his story, and Willard felt that this was another evidence of the power and blessing of God.

The old man set some food before him, a slice of cold pork and a corn cake, but although faint and weary, the new grave with that one name Harold in dismal black seemed in some strange way to fill his brain, choke his throat and burn in every vein. Indeed he could not keep his eyes from the open window and took no pains to hide his evident curiosity.

Seeing he ate nothing, the old man said apologetically, "The sojers tuk my cow, so I can't offer ye no milk."

After a pause, Willard asked, "Sir, might I ask if you know anything about the little occupant in yonder grave? I am curious to hear something about it."

The mountaineer stood with his canteen of water suspended while he searched the face of his questioner.

Without answering he went to the door, looked up and down the road and then quietly closed the door.

Coming back in he asked in a low voice, "Kin you tell me whar your sympathies run in this yere fight? Needn't be afeared to tell, I am no spy."

Willard returned the look fixed upon him and apparently satisfied, he presently replied, "I am no particular sympathizer with either party, sir, for my views and aims in life are strongly at variance with the shedding of blood. But if I were to tell the straight truth, I would say my heart is with the southern hosts, my life and associations have made it so."

"Stranger, we are nigh to the batteries of the 'ere party, but as I kin see from yer eyes and from yer clothes, ye air trustworthy, I kin tell yer I am a northerner, body and soul. How it comes that I am here is nuther here nor yonder. But seein's ye asked about the leetle grave out there, I sort o' feel like telling ye the hull story."

Filling his black pipe carefully and offering one to Willard, which was however refused, the old man again looked about his dooryard and again carefully closed the door.

"Thar's strange things happen in this yere war, and one o' the querest I've ever seen tuk place right hyar this very night just passed. I war purty sound asleep last night and I reckon it war after midnight when I heered all of a sudden a tremendous rappin' at my door; and when I asked who was there, a woman's voice answered back. So I got up, and there, shiverin' with fear or excitement was a woman and a leetle boy. Her niggers stood back with the horses, and all on 'em was in a purty bad fix, from ridin' so fast I reckon. Arter gettin' some supper, the woman, supposin', of course, as I was a Secesh told me that she was takin' the chile down to Richmond to put it into proper hands. The child looked scared and lonesome and seemed to be continually listenin'. Once in a while he would break out wi'a shout, 'It's a comin', it's a comin', it's nearly here'!"

"The old woman 'ud scold it then and command it to shet up. They were rich people I could tell by their clothes. I asked the woman once if the chile were hern, and with a clink of her jaws she said, "yes, he were'."

"They were to meet escorts in the mornin' and get aboard the train in the afternoon to go to Richmond. She was afeerd to go up onto the hill 'cause the danger of attack from Yankee boats. Part o' the night wore away, and she tried to sleep sittin' in her chair, but thet there chile's keepin' on with his shoutin' in his dose about 'them comin,' kept us all awake.

"At last about two o'clock this mornin' I hearn a shot. Then all hell war let loose, and such a poppin' and pingin' no one ever heard 'ceppin when bomb shells and batteries are a talkin' to each other.

"A northern ship I knew was out in the river and the batteries were a answerin' her salute. The woman war about crazy with fear, but I warn't much scared for we were so far off there war mighty little danger, and so I telled her.

"The first shot quieted down the boy, and he jest sot for nigh an hour in a corner, white and still.

"The woman 'ud screetch out bad wishes and what in a poor woman 'ud be called cusses on all northern rebels until my blood boiled and my hands tingled to slap her mouth. Fin'ly I could stan' it no more and I just went up to her and said, 'Missus, you jest shet that up, or by the livin' —— '

"At that instant the leetle boy gave one awful screech and made for the door, yellin',

"'It's comin', and it's yere.'

"Sure enough down through the air buzzing came one o' them turrible shells. I yelled too, and called to the chile. T'want no use; the ball struck the yarth about three rods from the boy, and piece which flew back from the awful hole made in the yarth caught the boy in the head, and – well, his own father 'uld never knowed who 'twas arter thet."

Slowly smoking a moment as if to forget the sad sight, the old man continued, "When he started, the old woman yelled, 'Harold, Harold, Harold!' Then round and round tore that woman a tarin' her har and clean gone crazy.

"I could see 'twar soon daylight and so I told the scared niggers to hop on their hosses and take the woman down to the railroad jest as fast as hoss-flesh could go, and they mighty soon lit out with their mistress a kickin' and screamin' in fine style.

"I knowed they had no time to lose, for from what I could jedge, the Yanks might soon be reinforced. When I got inside, I found the woman had left her satchel inside her chair –"

The old man went out again to listen, then coming back whispered, "Stranger, thet there satchel has about ten thousand dollars in jewelry in it. Well, not a dime of it gores to Richmond, but I guess ole Abe Lincoln 'uld tell something about it if he wants in," the sly wink of the old man's eye completed his sentence.

Willard had set paralyzed with the awful recital. He was too stupefied with horror to ask a question. He could not tell why he had been so affected, he dared not even ask his own heart why; but sat open-eyed and wretched watching the old man slowly refill his pipe.

"This mornin', soon as I could see a bit I went about and got them bits o' the child together and dug a grave over yender and writ on the headboard that name which the old woman war a yellin'."

After another pause the old man concluded, "I haint no call to tell this story, and I haint no call to keep it to myself. Yer hearn it now, seein' as ye was so curious, and I haint sorry I told it to ye."

It seemed an age before Willard could collect himself and overcome the horror that had settled down over him. His pale face, however, was no paler in comparison than the bronzed face of the mountaineer, and so excited no comment or surprise.

At last Willard managed to ask huskily, "Were there no souvenirs, no pictures, no mementos about the – the child (he could not say body, for there was no body left) or in the satchel, by which you could identify the child?"

Slowly withdrawing his pipe the old man said, "Stranger, you seem powerfully cut up about this yere thing. But arter all, thet's none o' my business. Yes, there was a pictur', and bein' as yer curious I don't mind showin' it to ye."

He arose slowly and going to a wooden chest in the corner, he drew out a good sized buckskin bag. Feeling about in its many and miscellaneous contents, he extracted a small pasteboard box. Coming up to Willard, he put it in his hands, and then went back to his seat and resumed his pipe. With a shaking hand, Willard drew a large gold locket from the box and even then hesitated long before he could control himself and open the spring.

He had felt it all along – but now – the locket contained the child's face, a lovely, sad-eyed child, and opposite, engraved on the lid, was the one word, "Randolph." Oh, what torture to find him here – and with a groan he rushed out into the open air and threw himself across the little grave with a heart-rendering cry of anguish.

It was quite an hour before he raised himself from the newly-made mound and dragged his limbs back into the cabin. The old man sat silently smoking, his rough furry cap pulled down a little lower over his eyes and a sad look in the lines about his mouth.

"Stranger," he said, "you seem terribly cut up over this yere new affair. Did ye know the chile?"

Willard told him he was certain as he could be that the poor boy was his own, only son, and begged the old man to let him have the locket to carry to the mother for certainty.

"Well, stranger, seein's I hev no pertic'lar right to it and you seem to hev, I'll let ye hev it. I don't keer to know anything more about the matter, though it do seem a trifle strange all through. Ye've no call to tell anyone 'bout my Yankee likings and I'se sure ye wouldn't 'fore I said anything to ye. I've seen many quar things in this war, and hearn many a yell of sufferin'. But yer little boy Harold –" how the name beat upon Willard's heart – "gin me the strangest feelin's I hev ever had."

It required little persuasion and less money to induce the old man to lend Willard his only horse, a swift-footed mountain pony, and with small delay, the wretched, heart-sore father sprang into the saddle and hurried on to Marysvale, conscious that there was need of his presence at that place.

Down the valley he rode, his heart like lead in his bosom, and ever and anon a bitter groan rising to his lips. This matter had cast his hopes almost to the earth. His boy dead, and such a death, his aunt crazed and fled no one knew where, how could he hope to find his wife or his friend?

Shudderingly, he remembered his wife's reckless wish that the child should die sooner than see its father's face.

How cruelly our wishes turn upon us when we think not!

He rode on, now fast, anon picking his way over fields planted with bones and graves instead of corn and cane. Occasional squads of skirmishers intercepted him, read his passports, and allowed him to proceed. But in no way could he shake off the awful gloom which, to his excited imagination, rested on every bush and twig. He was as if in a nightmare. He knew his horse was traveling, yet it seemed to him not one step forward was taken. The same trees, the selfsame hills, the very grass at his horse's feet seemed to be under the spell.

Almost he seemed to see the dark spirits of death and war, almost he seemed to hear the screech of the Avenging Angel as he swept along the sky. His hopes and anticipations had heretofore kept him cheerful amid all the desolation through which he traveled; but now, his heart torn asunder by the mountaineer's story, it seemed as if the nerves and sinews in his soul were bare to the touch of the brooding war angels of this blackened valley.

It was a high noon before Willard left the mountaineer's cabin, and he knew he had forty miles of hard riding between Aquia and Marysvale. It was a hot, sultry day, and his ankle gave him much pain and discomfort. He was compelled occasionally to stop and bathe the swollen limb in a creek or at a spring.

After a couple of hours, he noticed that his horse, too, seemed to limp and falter in the quick gallop he was urged to continue. This increased gradually, and it seemed to Willard as if every step of the limping pony was a fresh pang of anxiety and suspense to his overcharged heart.

"Well, old fellow," he said, patting the sweating horse, "have you, too, fallen under the horrible nightmare of accident, pain and anxiety which seems to be between me and my poor Hortense? What does it mean?"

"About four o'clock he halted beside a cool spring in a small grove to bathe his own swollen ankle and to do a similar office for his limping steed.

Just as he drew rein he heard a deep, quick "Halt!" and from behind a tree nearby saw the muzzle of a gun pointing at him. Without a tremor of fear, he calmly looked down the barrel of the gun and responded quickly, "Who are you?"

"Who are you?" was as quickly repeated by the concealed voice.

"A minister of the gospel in search of a wife in Marysvale. I have passports."

The soldier, with a blue coat, emerged from his hiding place and demanded the passport.

Willard was glad he had passports from the Federal Chief as well as his southern papers and carefully drew out the certificate.

"Is there a company of Union soldiers near by?" he asked.

After carefully reading the paper, folding it up and with a long, searching look into Willard's face, the soldier replied slowly. "Yes. Meade's Division is following up Lee's forces who are retreating down hereabouts."

"Is Meade's whole Division near here?" eagerly queried Willard.

"No, only a company in charge of the wounded. We are making our way down to a place near Warrenton, where we will find a house big enough for a war hospital. The main body of the army is ahead of us, and to the east."

"Do you know anything about the Twenty-seventh Pennsylvania Volunteers?"

"Yes, I know they were shot into hell at Gettysburg."

"There was a young man, Oscar Randolph was his name –"

"Well, comrade, I can't tell you anything about him or anyone else for I must move on."

Determined not to leave the grove until he had learned something further, Willard persisted, "I want to see your Captain. Where may I find him?"

"He is behind the ambulances, and if you will go down that lefthand road there, you will soon come upon the ambulances."

Willard turned his pony down the path or narrow road and as briskly as possible trotted away under the arching trees of the grove.

Once and again he gave and received the countersign as he passed two outriding soldiers, and then he met the first ambulance. He felt impelled to wait there until the heavy, noisy cars, full of suffering, groaning humanity had passed by him. Stopping his horse he uncovered his head and bowed with an indescribable, painful prayer for those wretches maimed and suffering for their country's dear sake.

The first one rolled heavily by. The second, just as it reached him, suddenly stopped; for the rotten wheel, striking against the trunk of a tree in the narrow path, snapped and was crushed into a hopeless mass of spokes and tire.

"What in hell's the matter now?" groaned a deep voice within the vehicle.

With a low cry, Willard jumped hastily down from his pony, and hopping and jumping reached the door of the ambulance. Tearing it open, he called, "Oscar Randolph?"

A pause, one of the sick men stretched out on the bottom of the car tried to lift his head, then fell back with a groan, "Is that Willard Gibbs or a ghost?"

Willard was not ashamed of the tears wrung from his eyes as he leaned over his friend Oscar and noted the changes time, war, suffering and pain had chiseled in Oscar's once handsome face.

The broken wheel was a serious affair away out in this lonely Virginian forest, and the two friends asked and answered each other's questions, forgetful for the moment of everything else. Poor Oscar had lost his leg at Gettysburg, and so badly had the surgeon done his work that it must be done all over at the gravest risk. Indeed Oscar tried to speak lightly, but his lips were pale when he told Willard he had only one chance in a thousand for life at all.

After some moments Willard's thoughts flew back to the lonely grave at Aquia, dug only that morning, and in horror-stricken tones he repeated the story to Oscar.

"If mother has run away from Oatland, that means that they have got an inkling of our intentions. I told our Captain about the old homestead and suggested that it be turned into a hospital. The news of our approach has been carried ahead for us by some spy."

"Well, I think I shall go back to the Captain and tell him what I have heard, for there may be word sent also to the southerners and that would mean a probable surprise or a skirmish at least."

So Willard again mounted his pony and hurried back to find the Captain of the small and broken company.

After pausing to allow the ambulances to file slowly ahead until they too reached the broken carriage, then to allow the file of weary, tramping soldiers to march past, he found the Captain riding easily along, chatting with his mounted companions.

Willard's breathless story with its probable contingencies roused the young Captain and he was at once alert and full of fire and eagerness.

"You say your pony is lame, Mr. Gibbs, and you wish to get there as soon as possible? Green, you go ahead to the broken ambulance and take out the roan horse from that team and help the gentlemen to exchange for his pony. Harvey, give the word along the line for a quick and an immediate march up to Oatlands. From what you say, Mr. Gibbs, we are still twenty miles from Marysvale, and it will be after midnight before we can possible reach there. We will leave all the ambulances here under a guard. I will send two mounted men ahead as scouts and you can either travel with them or alone as you choose."

Willard preferred being alone, for he felt he would be safer and more reliant on faith than on earthly help.

It did not take long to make the desired change, and with a stronger, better horse under him, he struck out on the road to Marysvale alone save for the angels of God which he had earnestly prayed might accompany him. His ankle was exquisitely painful, throbbing and swelling until he was almost distracted. Reaching a small stream running across the road, he dismounted, and going out of the public roadways, he crouched down under some bushes, bathed his foot and limb, and as he did so he fervently asked God to heal his sprain and cause the pain to cease and the swelling to go down. He had already cut his boot to allow the ankle room to swell, and after he had finished the ceremony, he again drew on his boot with less trouble than he dared hope and was soon in the saddle again.

Willard's road led through low hills and timber land, and he knew every inch of the way. The long summer twilight at last deepened into night, and he was still ten miles from Oatlands or from Marysvale.

How well he remembered the stately home of the Randolphs, the house situated on a rising knoll at the farther end of the valley or vale. The original two story building had received several additions, Mrs. Samual Randolph having added just before he and Hortense were married, a stately modern wing with a high imposing tower. The wing and tower were of lumber, and although artistically fashioned, looked like a tall, modern stylish wife beside a staid, stout, old fogy husband. The house was surrounded with terraced walks and flowers, while groves and orchards lay at the base of the knoll, the road from the gate leading up through a row of beautiful elms.

His own little home, a mile from the stately home of Mrs. Randolph, had been almost given away; and Willard hardly knew which memory was the stronger, the happiness of the first four months spent therein or the misery of the last two months when he had been alone and deserted.

With a whispered prayer for God to lead him not only to Hortense but also to her heart, he hurried along the soft, infrequent gleam of the tender new moon.

He was just at the top of the little ridge which divided the Marysvale from the Rose Valley when he thought he saw something skulking along under the pine tree at the roadside. He had refused to arm himself, feeling safer under the remembered prophecy of President Kimball than with a mounted army. So now, for a moment, he hesitated. Then in a loud, strong tone he called out, "Halt!"

"Oh, Lawd, deliber de chile!" came from the now prostrate figure under the trees.

"Whose nigger are you, and what are you doing here?" asked Willard, sternly.

"Oh marsa, I'se a po' ole man wifout eider fader or moder, not even a missis now, fo' she's runned away."

"Whose nigger are you?" again demanded Willard.

"I'se been bo'n and raised by Missy Randolph, but she's gone an' lef' us all alone."

"Michael, is it you?" asked Willard. "I thought your voice was very familiar."

"Yes, marsa, dat's de nane o' dis yere ole darky. Can yo' be po' Willie Gibbs, de boy who jined de Mo'mons and went to de debil?"

Without wasting time on explanations, Willard at once demanded to know what the old man was doing there, and how matters were in Oatlands.

"Befor' de Lawd," began the old man, trembling and crying pitifully, "I haint done nuffin 'bout it, fo' de Lawd, marsa. I'se runnin' clean away so I shan't have nuffin to do wif it."

It required a good deal of scolding and urging to get the old man to tell a straight story; but when he did get quieted down enough to talk, Willard's very soul was shaken with horrible dread.

Mrs. Randolph had told Hortense just as she was leaving the morning before that she had locked the boy Harold up in the top room of the tower with enough bread to last two days. This, Willard saw, was to throw Hortense on the wrong scent. The tower was found locked and barred with strong beams of wood. Hortense had ridden down to Warrenton and unable to find a carpenter who would go back with her she had procured tools and had spent the whole afternoon in tearing and pulling down lock after lock, barrier after barrier. Two or three faithful negroes had helped her in this work. A renegade negro, Samson, hearing that the Union Army was coming down through the valley thought it a good time for his scheme of revenge and plunder to be carried out; and so, as soon as night and weariness had compelled Hortense and her faithful adherents to get to bed for a few hours' repose, he had deliberately set fire to the tower; and while Hortense, crazed with grief and fright, banged vainly at the locked doors of the fast locked tower on the outside, he and two others had sacked and plundered the house, taking the few valuables left by Mrs. Randolph in her cruelly planned flight. This has not driven old Michael away, but when announced by shots and shouting, a company of rebel soldiers tore up the avenue towards the burning building, he had fled for his life.

Willard had dragged the story from the negro in quick gasps, and with a quickly smothered oath which rose so thoughtlessly to his lips, he dashed his spur into his horse and plunged forward in the darkness, his oath turned into an agonized prayer. Hortense, alone, surrounded by black devils, and as he bitterly thought "grey devils!" For he had seen and heard enough to know how little like men and how much like fiends men can be when filled with this spirit of rapine and plunder.

In a moment he had reached the summit of the hill, turned – yes – there, in the upper end of the vale, glowing like a witch's fire above the surrounding groves rose the awful gleam of the burning house. What horrible scenes might that glare be lighting in the shadow of those blackened walls!

This time a deeper, more agonized prayer, he threw himself fairly onto the neck of his flying steed and dashed down the valley road.

His head on the tightly grasped mane, his legs nearly on a line with his body, as he pressed close the quivering flank of the flying horse, he rode, skimming over the two miles that lay between the two points of the valley, the fire on the opposite hillside flaring redly against the trees.

The shadowy outlines of fences, fields, and cottages melted into the deeper obscurity of night and distance, the uncertain light of the young moon glancing out between dark, fleeting clouds. Sounds of commotion and excitement, lights glancing out from windows, forms of men or beasts he knew not which met him and pursued him, but he stopped not to call or question. It seemed as if a second was an hour and he never knew how few were the moments which his steed consumed in flying through the small, narrow vale until he found himself at Oatland gates; and at the sound of the distant shouting and yelling at the burning house, he remembered Oscar's words about the Southern Guerillas and realized these men were a desperate, reckless set, who would scarcely stop to enquire his name or business before shooting.

He could see the flames still ascending in jets over the trees, although dying away fast.

The heavy iron gate had been torn from its hinges and lay in the grass near the once trim little lodge. The light of the fire was sufficient to show him there were many moving forms both at the house and under the trees.

He stood a moment in indecision; he had turned into a bridle path that led by a rather circuitous route up to the house, and held his panting horse a moment while he wondered and prayed as to his next movement.

As he stood, he fancied he heard a scream above the confused din. It was strangely muffled, if it was a scream, but even as he doubted, the very elm trees caught and trembled at the shrill cry of "Help, mur –" cutting the darkened air with a sharp, keen sound. It was a woman's voice, that woman – Hortense.

With an answering shout of careless horror, Willard dashed through the path and only paused as he reached the confines of the grove. He was in the dense shadow made by the firelight and friendly trees, and his eyes traveled instantly over the burning, smoking ruins of the frame wing and once stately tower, the solid firm rock building untouched save as to windows and doors by the destroying element. A score or so of men swarmed in and out of the building, adding to the heaps of plunder outside every movable article in the house. Hortense was not at the house.

Piercing the surrounding gloom as keenly as he could, he still saw no trace of her.

Again, not so loud, but more agonized, rang out that piteous cry for help. Guided by the sound, his eyes caught the gleam of white on the opposite side of the grove, and as a jet of flame suddenly spurted up from the almost dying fire, he distinctly saw a man struggling with and dragging off into the dense shadows of the wood, a woman – the white gleam of clothes, her loose night robe.

Forgetting everything but the fire in his brain and the murderous desire that clinching his throat and stiffened his fingers, he flung himself from his horse and started for the spot.

His ankle? He flung off both his boots, feeling he should thus be stronger, and then knowing well that to show himself to the renegades and desperados at the fire would be to court instant death, he flung himself swiftly through the underbrush of the forest or grove which skirted the knoll, his heated breath hissing through his set teeth in quick gasps.

Could he, hampered by the long circuit, the darkness and his weak ankle, reach the other side in time? This flashed through his mind. His ankle! It was no longer weak; he took no thought or question why but tore his way along regardless of thorns or briars.

He could see nothing in the dense shadows, and he scarcely knew which way to turn; even as he hesitated, he fancied he saw a fleck of white on a distant bush. Yes, it was a bit of lace torn by a passing briar from the woman's gown. And here, this must be the path, a narrow footpath leading down to a secluded spring he remembered well.

Noiselessly he fled, his stockinged feet on the grassy path, his hands clinched and unclinching themselves in awful longing.

A growl of rage, a low muttered curse from a black shadow near a gleam of white upon the grassy sward close to the faintly glistening spring, the horrid sound of a blow on some soft yielding substance, and Willard sprang upon the prostrate shadow, and there was a fierce, silent, short struggle, and then –

The closely clinched hands of the outraged husband had left a blue wicked streak around the burly throat of the vile wretch who had been surprised and thus left at his assailant's mercy. Jumping off from the huge form of his now silent victim, Willard struck him viciously in the head, careless for the moment as to the result.

With a sob in his throat, he turned to the equally silent form of the woman and knelt down beside her.

The soft moonbeams sometimes penetrated through the thick curtain of leaves, but not sufficiently to aid him in his quick and anxious searchings. He felt he knew it was his wife, and yet he wished he was able to satisfy his eyes of this fact.

He drew his hands over her hair, the same long, soft tresses, the pretty ears, the soft slender throat; but her face! It was wet, very wet. He had wetted his hands too in this liquid on her face; and her features – certainly were not like Hortense, the nose so large, the cheeks so protuberant. Suddenly he remembered, as by a flash, the oath of anger, the sound of the blow given no doubt by the villain near by. Why, he had struck her in the face! That was why her features were swollen. The wet – was blood! Oh, had he found his wife to only find her dead body!

He put his hand over her heart to see if it still beat. Poor child! Her slight robe had been torn into shreds during her fierce struggle with her assailant, and her cold, lifeless form was uncovered save for the long silken tresses which swept around her like a veil. He could feel no heart beat. He put his face down near the cold bosom, and his cheek met the loved form with a thrill of deepest anguish.

Yet no – there surely was a faint flutter under his cheek, the heart had not ceased its life throbs! With tender swiftness he raised the lovely form in his arms and gently laid her down on the edge of the spring. He poured great handfuls of the cool liquid onto the swollen face and over the throat and bosom.

He sought the hands to chafe and bathe them. They were tightly clenched. He unclasped the fingers.

"Poor, helpless child!" he half sobbed as he found bits of flesh and some hairs in the hands dug from the face of the wretch whom she had so bravely sought to repel.

"God bless thee, and give thy life back to me that I may protect and cherish thee forevermore," he murmured as he rubbed and bathed the bruised and bleeding face and hands.

He knew she was still alive from the occasional flutter in her throat, but she remained utterly unconscious in spite of all his efforts. At last her breathing became assured, yet she lay passive as in a deep stupor.

Rising, he drew off his coat and wrapped it about her, rightly guessing that the dampness had perhaps chilled the delicate frame.

Turning instinctively to the prostrate wretch near the spring, he stooped and felt his pulse to know if he had killed or only stunned him. There was certainly a slight beating of his pulse, and then he sprang to the silent form of his wife, and picking her up he carried her with some difficulty several rods into the underbrush where they would be concealed while night lasted.

He began to realize that his own body had been severely taxed. The terrible experience at Aquia Creek, his accident, loss of sleep and the many exhausting events of the last twenty-four hours had begun to tell upon him.

Yet even as he sat chafing the hands of his wife, he heard the murmur of approaching voices, and he again picked up his heavy burden and as quickly as might be plunged still further into the forest.

It was well that he did so, for even as he fled he heard two shots, shouts, and then he knew the Union soldiers must have arrived, and there was a fierce skirmish between them and the reckless band of Guerilla plunderers who had sacked the deserted homestead.

Bullets came dangerously near where Willard crouched even as it was, for some of the Guerillas had evidently fled down the path taken by Willard in his pursuit of his wife and her abductor.

After a time the firing ceased, and, waiting a short time longer, Willard left his still unconscious wife and cautiously ventured near the entrance to the forest. Yes, the Union soldiers had arrived and had evidently routed the mountain desperados, for they were busily engaged, Willard could plainly see by the light of two huge bonfires, in putting out the smoldering fire, carrying into the store part of the house all of the furniture and various articles so recently piled up by the Guerillas.

Obtaining some quilts and a shutter, Willard asked one of the soldiers to accompany him and together they brought up to the house the still unconscious woman. As they passed the spring, Willard was relieved to know the body of his victim had been removed, and in the cooler moment of deliberation he was not sorry to hope that he had not stained his hands with the blood of murder, albeit so justifiable if the man had really been dead.

All that night Willard worked and rubbed and watched over his wife. He had taken her up to Mrs. Randolph's chamber which had been in the old part of the house; and as the dim light of the candle showed him the grim faces of the dead and gone Randolphs, he thought sorrowfully of the wretched state to which pride, prejudice and this Civil War had reduced the remaining descendants of a haughty, wealthy race of aristocrats.

The swollen features of the figure upon the bed could scarcely be recognized as those of his once beautiful wife. His heart failed him lest the shock and the constant strain of exciting events had either sapped the springs of life or would affect the reason of the wife he had so dearly rescued.

As he bent over her chafing her hands, the memory of President Kimball's prophecy drifted into his mind, and it flashed all over him like the shock of an electric battery, "I am to return with my lamb to the fold."

"Thank God for the blessed prophecy and the happy memory of it," he whispered, kneeling down at the bedside.

Recalling the miraculous healing of his own aching, swollen limb at the wayside spring, he took some water in his hand and asking God to hear his fervent prayer, he bathed the swollen cheeks and nose and rebuked the swelling, pain and inflammation. He had no way of procuring consecrated oil, but he administered to her by virtue of his priesthood and felt to prophesy that she would receive the gift of healing, insomuch that her delicate flesh should loose all marks and stain of the spoiler's hand.

His mind was still, however, on a cruel strain, and it was with a feeling of intense relief that he saw, a short time after daylight, the lids of her eyes slowly uplift and her eyes fastened upon him in a confused state.

Her first words drove the blood to his heart with a sickening fear that she had lost her reason.

"Am I dead?" she whispered slowly.

He leaned over her speechless with misery.

"You have come to carry me; where are you going to carry me? I have just been into the black void men call hell."

"Hortense, it is I, your living husband. Don't be frightened, darling."

"Have you brought Harold? Oh, he is in the tower; let me go, let me go – don't you hear –"

He held her down while he whispered soothing words into her ear.

After a time she grew calmer and seemed to slowly gather the fact that Willard was a living being, and she grew momentarily calmer and more peaceful as this happy fact distilled itself throughout her bruised and bleeding consciousness. At last she fell quietly asleep, holding his arm in her close clasp, his face near her cheek and his warm breath in her neck as he whispered soft blessings of peace and comfort to her drowsy ears.

Willard himself dropped wearily off to sleep, and for the first time for two nights he slept a heavy, dreamless sleep.

It was late; he must have slept on for hours, for his first consciousness was a deep sigh uttered by Hortense as she sought to move her arm from its cramped position.

"My husband," she said softly and in a low, mournful voice, "how did you come here? Where is Harold? Where did you find me?"

He was awake at once, and putting his arms around her trembling form he told her all of the sad, sorrowful story that he felt was wisdom for her to know. After, he asked the one absorbing question that had so bitterly tormented him since he had found her unconscious by the spring.

"Patsey, my poor darling, tell me, your husband, was I in time, in time to save the one thing more precious than life itself, the honor of my wife?"

"Oh yes, Willard, indeed you were; for I lost consciousness only when he struck me in the face. Oh, Will, if you had not come!" and she clung to him in a shivering fit of well remembered terror.

After a few words of comforting assurance, Willard arose from his cramped position on his knees and hurried downstairs to get water and food for Hortense and for his own exhausted body.

Part XIV

That day was one of the three eventful days which burned themselves into both Willard's and Hortense's minds with a vividness never to be wiped out through time or eternity.

The ambulances arrived towards evening, and Hortense insisted on arising and arranging the habitable rooms of the house with all the comfort possible for the sick and suffering heroes. She gave her own spacious room to her loved cousin Oscar, and together she and Willard arranged every comfort for the young man.

Hortense was surprised to find she felt so little inconvenience from the terrible blow she had received on her face and often spoke to Willard about it, calling his attention to the swift abatement of the swelling and redness. He said nothing of the cause thereof, feeling it better to wait until she knew something of the gospel and its power.

Hortense was installed by the army surgeon at once as chief nurse, the men detailed therefore being her willing but awkward assistants.

Oscar's condition was very doubtful, and the doctor sought to build up his general health before undertaking the second amputation.

"Will," Oscar said the second day, as he lay restless and weary, "bring your Book of Mormon and read it to me."

Delighted with the request, Willard drew the precious book from his pocket where it was always carried along with a small pocket Testament, and choosing some comforting passages in the sayings of the Savior he read until the sick man's eyes closed in quiet sleep.

This was the first, but by no means the last time that Willard read and explained the beautiful principles of this glorious gospel, and Willard's ardent hope was more than realized by the ardent way in which his friend sought and obtained the knowledge so dear to the honest heart. Especially was he delighted with the principle of redemption of the dead, it seemed so broad, so noble, so Christ-like to his hungry soul.

"When I'm gone," he would say to Willard in his old, careless way, "you can do my business up for me just as well as if I had done it myself; better, too," he would always add with a touch of sad bitterness in his tone.

Willard sought with all the strength of his own earnest hope to install faith and hope into the heart of his beloved friend. It was useless. Oscar declared he should die. Willard taught him the principle of healing and often administered to him, but he felt in his own soul that there was small room for hope.

Willard was very anxious to include Hortense in the various conversations he held with Oscar on religious subjects, and whenever possible she seemed a pleased if quiet listener to all the talk.

The severe illness of Oscar, which chained Willard to his side save for short intervals of rest, as well as the heavy and constant labors of Hortense in the many sick chambers of this new hospital, prevented the two from having one moment's conversation alone together. So that insensibly Willard's anxiety lest Hortense should again refuse to go with him when she learned he had another wife in Utah, and her wonderment at the seeming half-indifference of his manner towards her, caused an apparent estrangement between husband and wife.

"Mrs. Gibbs," said the doctor one morning about two weeks after their arrival, "you can prepare Mr. Randolph for the operation which must take place tomorrow. I dare not delay it a single hour after that."

"Very well," said Hortense, white to the very lips with distress and agitation; "Is there hope?"

"I can only answer by repeating that ancient medical truism, "while there's life there's hope," replied the surgeon gravely.

In a few quiet words the necessary information was given to the two friends, and Oscar was the only calm, collected one of the three after the announcement had been made.

"You two must not feel like this; aren't you afraid you will shake my nerves?" he asked banteringly.

Willard and Hortense exchanged guiltily mournful glances at their forgetfulness, and then Willard began to speak of the great chain of eternity of which this sad, old time is but a link, a rusty, often jagged link, but it joins into the grand chain which men call eternity.

"That's a glorious thought, old boy, that there is no standstill to progression, no stopping place for intelligence. To feel that even after we have reached the great place occupied by our Father in heaven we shall find Him still far in advance of us in the grand march of progress. Your religion is as broad as eternity and as deathless as love." After a pause he added, "Bury me quietly here where all my fathers lie, and when you reach Utah, do all that you can for me."

Willard read to him quietly then for some time.

"Oscar," he said, shortly after Hortense had brought in the solitary tallow candle – lights of all kinds were hard to obtain in those war times – "I wish I could persuade you to look on the bright side of this question. I know, I have proven, that one's own faith and hope have much to do with our living and dying. The principle of faith is very far-reaching, and it is as much a law subject to understanding and to control as is the law of baptism. Cheer your own spirits up and all may yet go well with you, and I can yet have the pleasure of baptizing you into the truth."

"No, Will, it is not to be. I feel that I am to die, and I am glad that it is so. Let me make a confession. I rather dread the thought of getting well and facing the ridicule of friends if I accepted Mormonism. And I know Mormonism is true. Yes, dear old Will," as he felt the pressure of his friend's affectionate handclasp, "I can understand and appreciate the intense love of this gospel which enabled you to forsake friends, home and a lovely wife for the hope of that pure and holy religion. But I am not as morally brave as you are – hush – don't expostulate – it is very true – and I might not have the courage to come out and dare the sneers of my friends."

"Can you, who lie hero for a cause, call yourself a coward?"

"Yes, Will, I am a coward. It don't take as much courage to go out to fight, applauded by everyone, even approved of by your own vanity, and go with thousands of others to a probable death surmounted by a halo of glory. But it does make a man wince to be sneered at and scorned by all those whose good opinion he values. It's no use, Will, I'm only a failure after all, in my own, my mother's and even God's eyes. What matter, I shall be called my 'country's defender' and that is some consolation."

Willard sat with his hands over his aching eyes and presently the sick man stirred again. Hortense came in just then and she went to the bedside and knelt down quietly.

"Don't feel bad, folks, please; it's all right. God does all things all right. Say, Hortense, I want to say just a word to you. Don't ever let anything come between you and Will again. No matter how you may feel, nor what he may think, it is his duty to do. Stick to him through thick and thin, just as you promised when you married him. He's worthy of it, dear girl; we've proven that."

"Oh, Oscar, I mean to be true to him," said the wretched girl as she bowed her head over her hands but feared to give way to her grief lest it might agitate her cousin.

Willard stroked the bowed head and was deeply stirred at the humble admission from the once reserved and proud girl.

"Willard," Oscar said again, "I have been man enough to ask God to give me an assurance of the truth of what you have told me, and I want to tell you that He has answered my prayers. He has not sent me a vision, I am not a fit subject perhaps for so great a testimony, but He has given to my soul a sweet, peaceful hope and reliance, a firm belief in every principle you have taught me that is an invincible proof to me that Mormonism is true. I am so glad, for it's balm to my soul."

The sick man seemed to find relief in thus unbosoming his inmost thoughts to those two loved ones on this night which he felt was his last upon earth.

"I have never been a very wicked man, Will, and it is a comfort to know I shall be rewarded for the few good deeds I have done, while I shall not suffer for that which I was helpless to prevent."

He lay then a long while in the sputtering candle light. Presently Willard bethought himself of that lovely hymn by E. R. Snow, "O My Father," and although not much of a singer, the beautiful, soul-inspiring words and the intense sympathy which his own feelings gave to the song made it glorious to the sick man, even beyond the expression of words.

> O my Father, thou that dwellest
> In the high and glorious place!
> When shall I regain thy presence
> And again behold thy face?
> In thy holy habitation
> Did my spirit once reside;
> In my first primeval childhood,
> Was I nurtured near thy side.
>
> I had learned to call thee Father
> Through thy Spirit from on high;
> But, until the Key of Knowledge
> Was restored, I knew not why.
> In the heavens are parents single?
> No; the thought makes reason stare!
> Truth is reason, truth eternal,
> Tells me I've a mother there.
>
> When I leave this frail existence
> When I lay this mortal by
> Father, mother, may I meet you
> In your royal court on high?
> Then at length when I've completed
> All you sent me forth to do
> With your mutual approbation
> Let me come and dwell with you.

When the last note died away, the sufferer sighed as if in sweet resignation and soon after fell into a half stuper or doze.

The next morning Willard and Hortense took their places on each side of the long table, and just before having the chloroform applied Oscar whispered to Willard, "Don't forget me when you get to Zion."

Those were his last words! In three hours from that time Willard drew down the eyelids and composed the features of his dead friend, for the hand of the death angel had grasped the heart of the hero, and one more life had been offered on the altar of duty and country!

Both Willard and Hortense were so overcome with grief for days that a shadow rested over every detail of life. The death of a loved one seems to cloud the mind no less than the heart with a sense of utter hopelessness.

As Willard's mind began to grasp again the realities of life he felt he had a difficult and severe task before him. Hortense did not dream that he had another wife; indeed she had, as I have heretofore remarked, already secretly wondered why her husband was so careful to treat her with a distant affection that held no hint of wedded relations. The poor, proud girl interpreted it in her own way, and flew to the conclusion that Willard thought her now unworthy of him, and unfit to be his wife because of the sad experience in the grove. She grew into a state of brooding melancholy over the matter, which prevented her from observing Willard who was as sad and as silent as she, but from a different cause.

Days, weeks passed in this wretched way, until both were becoming almost useless. Neither slept nor ate much, and each saw the other's increasing palor with a sad misunderstanding of the cause. Both were taxed to the utmost with the heavy labors of the hospital, and Hortense was really almost exhausted.

Willard had been there nearly a month and knew if he was to get back to Utah that fall he had no time to lose.

One night he reached a resolve. He was not brave nor wise enough to teach Hortense this strange principle, he thought, but he would fast and pray for three days that God might show her His tender mercy.

That day he managed to absent himself from meals without exciting comment, but that night he took his blankets into the woods below and spent most of the night in struggling prayer. The next day he again escaped comment from all but Hortense who asked him where he was at dinner time. His confused reply and quick turning to another subject roused her curiosity, and she watched him at suppertime.

She was too proud to question him again, but wondered within herself what this phase of conduct could mean? Was he deliberately starving himself to death? This could not be, for she was the one who should die, not he.

Suddenly she remembered hearing him tell Oscar how the Mormons believed in the ancient mode of receiving answers to prayers. Was Willard fasting? And for what? She could not even conjecture. But after much reflection, she decided to be a party to that fast, no matter what its object.

Nothing could better prove the softening influence which trouble and influence had produced on the hitherto defiant heart of Hortense than this little incident. I do not say that trouble and misery will soften all proud hearts, sometimes they seem to dull and harden such souls; but Willard's prayers had prevailed in the heavens, and his wife's heart had been in the hand of God.

The second night was also spent in the knoll-forest by Willard, and he felt already a lifting of his burden. The next day his eyes seemed to be clearer. He seemed to pierce through the veil of his own anxiety and to see the pale, beloved, faced of his wife, grown strangely haggard and wan. What was the cause? Why was she brooding? Dimly he wondered if he had anything to do with it, or was it the child, or even Oscar's death? Slowly for him the veil between them was lifting, and his heart was instructed.

To Hortense this day of fasting was a very new experience. But as the hours slipped by she seemed to have a clearer comprehension of her husband and to know that he, too, was suffering, but not from repugnance to her. When the two would catch each other's glances, there was a mutual soul-cry exchanged for a better understanding, a nearer relation.

That night, the third night of Willard's fast, after he had gone away from the house, Hortense watched him go down the path toward the dense growth of trees which she so shuddered to even glance at, and she stole away to her chamber and kneeling down humbly asked for light, and for the blessing to be given to her husband which he desired.

Then she hurried to her sick and suffering soldiers. At last her night arrangements were all made, and she took up her night watch beside a fevered patient who required periodical attentions.

The hours slipped by. She had in her hands a pamphlet which Willard had given her, and after some time she read its title. It was a sermon on the Eternity of the Marriage Covenant. She knew by this time that Mormons believed in the patriarchal order of marriage, but her natural repugnance had prevented her seeking any further knowledge on the subject.

The sermon was a powerful one by Elder John Taylor, and she grew more and more interested. Her patient was better and slept between the times for medicine pretty quietly. At last, about one o'clock, after trimming the candle and arranging her patient again on his pillows, she dozed in her chair. Ten, fifteen, twenty minutes passed, and then she sprang up out of her chair with a low, happy cry.

Everything was just as she had left it, and she sat a moment, tears streaming down her face and lost in deep reverie. Just then one of the nurses came to relieve her for the night, and she went swiftly and quietly down the wide stairway out to the front door.

The porch was bathed in the soft, July moonlight, and as she opened the door and stood upon the threshold her husband was upon the terrace steps.

His pale face glowed in the white light, his dark eyes seemed brighter than stars, and he questioned softly, "Patsey, have you come for me?"

"Yes, oh, yes," as she sprang into his arms. "O, my husband, I am so happy, so happy."

They sat down in the calm midnight stillness and listened a moment to the soft and distant sound of the sentry's clanking step.

They were alone and safe from interruption or from listening ears.

Part XV

"My husband, I have been to Heaven." The strange words, the impossible fact, which at another time might have either shocked or excited Willard's ridicule, now fell upon his ears like music for he had received in the grove a testimony that his long prayer had been answered, and now behold it was so!

"At least, my spirit has," went on her happy voice as they sat on the stone steps of the piazza.

"I have been sitting up tonight at poor Karkin's bedside and the last time I looked at the clock it was just one o'clock. Then I forgot everything about my surroundings. I was in a dark valley, and a personage dressed in a loose, white robe stood afar up on the hillside. I seemed to hear his voice whisper 'come,' but my feet were mired in the clay of the valley. 'Can I come?' I called. 'If you will,' was answered. With a mighty effort I tore myself from the clay and then began to ascend so easily, so swiftly. But my feet, I seemed to know, were torn and bleeding from the struggle I had made and were now bared of both shoes and stockings. As soon as I reached the angel's side, he took my hand and we soared up, up, up. Sometimes past worlds with beings like earth's children, past suns, whose glaring brightness would have shriveled me like old parchment but for the touch of the angel's hand. Then we reached a lovely globe inhabited by white, shining spirits. Such exquisite delight as brooded, fathoms deep, like an atmosphere, over every lovely scene! I have no words, oh, what are words to describe the glories of that place! But most of all, I saw and sensed the heavenly peace and love which shone on every countenance. And as I gazed more steadily, the lovely forms of the inhabitants there seemed to be those of little children, of infants! I cannot describe the peculiar effect made upon my mind. If I opened my eyes wide and stared, it seemed as if they were children, but when I grasped my guide's hand and looked, as it were from his eyes, they were full-grown beautiful spirits. I knew instinctively that they were spirits, for there was a light, ethereal quality about them that told me what they were. How my heart thrilled with a strange, unaccountable longing as I looked upon them! I could not comprehend my own sensations. And once as I looked down at my bare and bleeding feet, I saw they were all healed and shone with white brightness."

"My angel guide was silent, and I forbore to question him. At last the sporting, happy creatures nearest us seemed to become conscious of our watching presence. They communicated in some swift way I did not understand our presence to others far off. The grassy glade wherein we stood was watered by a silvery, clear stream. As I gazed about full of love and longing, a beautiful form approached us, on the other side of the stream, and looking with silent longing straight at me, the shape reached out a pair of pleading arms as if to beg me to clasp it to my bosom. As my eyes were opened wide, it was an infant, Willard, and its hair and eyes were so like yours I could have died to hold it in my arms. The sad memory of my own lost Harold seemed to become absorbed, swallowed up as it were in the exquisite longing I felt to reach and clasp that pleading form to my bosom. I cannot even describe the heavenly love of it all. Then others, I counted four, six, eight, or even more, floated to that other one and returned to me my gaze of love and longing.

"I cannot describe the heavenly love and yearning which filled me with infinite bliss as I stood so silently watching those lovely beings. I could bear this silence no longer, and turning to my guide I implored him to tell me who and what these beings were. Even as I spoke our feet left the heavenly shore and we were softly soaring, or, rather, floating through a silent space."

"'Those beings,' answered my guide, 'are those spirits reserved by the Mighty Father to come forth in the last days through the lineage of the patriarchal marriage. They are the chosen seed spoken of by the Nephite Jacob!!'"

"'Are they unborn?' I cried, my heart springing instantly to the lovely child-face across the stream."

"'Yes.'"

"'And may I not bring some of them into the world?' I asked again emboldened by his manner."

"'It is your privilege, if you are humble and faithful. But know this, your heart will be torn and bleeding with earthly woes even as your feet were lacerated in the valley!'"

"Then he turned his flight earthward, and knowing he must soon leave me I hastened to ask, 'And was that heaven?'"

"'A part of heaven. For heaven is as wide as space, as far-reaching as eternity'."

"Our feet were on the hillside we had left, and with a whispered warning, 'Beware of pride,' I was alone and at once awoke. The tears were streaming from my eyes with joy. Oh, Willard, can it be that this thing I have dreaded, this plural marriage, will it bring us so much happiness as flooded my whole being?"

Patiently he told her all he could, taught her the worthy and beauty of the eternal covenant. He also told her of the many trials met by weak mortals in trying to subdue the human heart. Then without a fear he told her of his wife Aseneth and baby girl, and she, taught by suffering and visited by mercy, was a willing pupil in this school.

Still another task lay before him, that of explaining to her how, under that new law, she was not yet his wife. Not until they were in Zion and had been sealed over the alter would she be his wife or he her husband. He considered it best to have the whole matter finished that night, and so went on explaining the whole principle to her. She listened quietly, and if a trembling of the sensitive mouth occasionally betrayed her, at least there were no hardened lines of pride or resentment. After he finished his talk, she sat a minute, then putting her head down on his shoulder and drawing his ear down to her lips she whispered, "You do not despise me for that – that horrible night?"

"Oh, Patsy, how, my darling, how could you imagine such a wicked thing? You surely know better."

After a few more whispered explanations she again asked, "And you will love me quite as well as –"

"Ever?" he hurried finished for her, dreading comparisons. "Better, a thousand times better. Never in my life did I love you so well as at this moment, be sure of that."

After a few moments' reflection as if to weigh well his words, he said, "Hortense, I can safely say, I never loved any woman better than I do you, and I am sure I can promise you I never will. Does that satisfy you?"

"Yes," with a little sigh, for this new order of things already held her clogged like clay in the valley. "I ought to be satisfied." Then suddenly, lifting her head, she exclaimed, "One thing sure, my husband, I never loved and respected you so much in my life as I do now. I would forsake everything on earth to be by your side. And what is strange, you seem some way to have grown so big mentally and morally that I am content to be obedient to you. Really, Will," with a half smile, "I don't believe there are many men like you, even in Utah."

Was not this glorious recompense for all the faithful husband's struggles and prayers? He thought so. And when for the first time in his life, he that night asked Hortense to kneel with him on the silent piazza and unite in family prayers, he felt as if he had received a taste of heaven's own glory in this perfect reconciliation.

In speaking next day about going out to Utah, Hortense begged Willard not to urge her to leave her post of duty beside the sick and suffering soldiers, nor did she wish baptism until safe in Zion's borders.

After much consultation, it was agreed that they should both wait till spring before trying to get away. It was doubtless too late to join any returning mission companies, and Willard thought by going up to Philadelphia or Washington he could get a situation for the winter and earn some money to pay the Bishop as well as to help his family along.

Accordingly he wrote a detailed account of the matter to the First Presidency, the Bishop and Aseneth.

Then, after doing all he could to make Hortense comfortable, he set out on his return trip to Washington.

His journey was void of any exciting incidents, and he did not even get near Aquia Creek. He had, of course, told Hortense about the sad grave, and the miniature proved beyond a doubt that their beloved child had been slain. It seemed a relief to the mother to know this, for now her fears and doubts were at rest concerning him. His little mind had certainly been injured by the strain of war and warring elements of those around him, and the mother spent more peaceful moments in gazing fondly at the picture and knowing the child was at last at rest than she had known for two years.

Again in Washington the kind offices of Captain Hooper were exercised in Willard's behalf, and he found a very lucrative position as a bookkeeper in a dry goods store.

Willard's mission experiences had taught him the useful lesson that life could be very comfortably sustained on good bread and an occasional treat of vegetables and fruit. It was a blessing to him now, for although his wages were extremely good, yet his expenses were proportionally large. However, his frugal habits saved his pennies, and he easily took care of his gold dollars.

His one luxury was stationary. This he would have. And so, both Aseneth and Hortense had the pleasure of receiving long and frequent letters from the lover-husband.

Sometimes, when he found a chance, he would send some trifling gift down to Hortense. Such gifts as a pair of shoes, a few yards of cloth or a paper of pins and needles. Such gifts as young ladies now-a-days would consider too trifling for gratitude. But they meant, not only great comfort to the recipient in those days, but quite an outlay of money to the sender.

Willard pleased himself one day by buying two good trunks; and into one of these which was designed for Aseneth, he carefully laid away the duplicate of every article which he sent to Hortense.

This was the result of much study and reflection on his position. He resolved that the very best course for him to pursue in his family relations was to be strictly just and impartial even to the smallest detail. I do not particularly advocate his course as best for every man to follow, but certainly after watching him and his family for years I think his way the wisest and most righteous course I have ever seen pursued.

With a delicious ignorance of women's wear generally, he would carefully purchase seven yards of print each for a dress, and in the selection of ribbons his taste was something fearful. And, too, after careful deliberation, he would buy shoes two sizes smaller for Aseneth then for Hortense because Hortense was the taller of the two. In reality, Aseneth's foot was several sizes larger than Hortense's. However, the things were all godsends to those for whom they were designed and most thoroughly appreciated.

In the winter near Christmastime, he received a package from Aseneth. It contained two abrotype pictures in pretty, black, velvet-lined cases. One was of herself and the little one; the other contained the baby's face alone. The first, her letter told him, was taken for "dear papa." The second was from "baby Hortense to aunty."

What a thoughtful girl Aseneth was! And with what delight did he gaze upon the calm, noble features with the little one nestling close up to her cheek.

Aseneth always sent kind messages to the young wife in Virginia so patiently working out her way to "salvation" and sometimes Hortense replied with a few kind but distant words of response.

That picture of the baby was a happy thought. Willard at once sent it on to Hortense explaining that he had neglected to tell her the child had been christened for her. When Hortense opened it, a faint thrill of – yes – it was certainly love, even if tinged with pain, crept over her. As she gazed, she seemed to see a faint resemblance to those spirit faces. The babe had, at the moment it was taken, thrown out its arms in playful eagerness, and to the eyes of Hortense, it seemed as if the baby eyes gazed longingly into hers. She was conquered. She kissed the glass again and again, and passionately wondered if this were the child spirit of her vision and if she should never again be a mother. However, she resolved to love the child and to love her mother for the child's and Willard's sake.

What a lifting of her feet out of the clay came with that resolve! It is so much easier to do right, to feel right, when we want to do so!

Nurses came to the hospital during the winter, and early in the spring Hortense gathered her few personal effects together and prepared to go up to Washington with the party of soldiers who were returning on sick leave. Willard was not able to leave and come down for her, and she did not wish it, for she was brave and capable.

Willard had made all arrangements to leave with the first company of emigrants to the valley in the early spring, and to avoid questions and comments, she was to travel as his cousin, Miss Randolph.

I do not deny that there was quite a trial to both these loving hearts in this firm stand they had taken. Nor do I deny that a flitting whisper would sometimes suggest to Willard that this sweet woman he held in his arms to kiss good night was his wife in the eyes of men and would be soon in the eyes of angels. But he was noble enough to recognize and repel the tempter, and with a hurried movement he would put her away and retire to his own room and lonely couch.

It was suffering to them both. Such suffering though as steadies every heart string and tightens the hand upon the iron rod of truth and self control.

When Patsey saw the other trunk and recognized the duplicated articles which had given her so much pleasure, there was a sudden tightening round her heart. She stood looking down into the trunk with stormy eyes.

"What is it, Patsey," said Willard coming into the room, "are your feet sinking down again into the mire of the dark valley? Come, look up."

She did, and after a few moments she had overcome that temptation. Indeed, she afterwards took great pleasure in buying other needed articles to lay in this trunk and would sometimes protest when Willard insisted on her having the same for herself.

We will not follow the "cousins" on the long journey across the plains but merely say they were rejoiced when they found themselves away from the horrid excitement and sights caused by the raging Civil War.

The joy Willard felt when he stood at the mouth of Emigration Canyon and looked down into his beloved "Zion" was shared by Hortense. She was so glad and happy to be at last in peace and with a strong, true heart to lean upon.

Trees had grown, fences and barns were far more plentiful, houses had sprung up, and miles of smiling fields had crowded out the gray, forbidding sage brush in the three years of Willard's absence.

Their wagon was the fourth or fifth in the long train, and they did not see a flying horseman approaching the train until he passed them, peering closely at them as he rode.

"It is them. Will, hi! Don't you know me?" called the youth as he wheeled quickly back after that glance of recognition.

Then Willard sprang out and fairly hugged the tall, ungainly form of Tommy Mainwaring who had come out to meet him.

"You are to come straight to our house; Aseneth and the baby, Aunt Sarah and her girls, besides the whole Mainwaring tribe are there assembled," said Tommy breathlessly.

Willard had hurriedly clambered back into the wagon, and after a few hasty words of introduction between Tom and Hortense, he whipped up his jaded horses into a lively trot and they passed the other wagons, leaving surprise and a long line of unwelcome dust behind them.

Tommy trotted along beside them and regaled them with sundry bits of home and town gossip.

"Lou's been married, you know, a year, and five weeks ago she turned over a new leaf and began life as a mother. Mighty fine youngster. I tell you Joe Miller is a proud father. Aunt Sarah? Alack is me! Two more girls since you left. So you see her sun is still unrisen. It'll come up some day yet, maybe. Anyhow there's a whole raft of salvation earners in that quarter for some man. Rone's married too. They are down at Provo, have located there. But we're expecting them up today to see you. Rhoda? Oh! She's hung her harp on a willow tree, I guess. She's smashed lots of hearts since you went away, but her own seems pretty sound as yet."

The youth rattled on, and so did the wagon until at last the old familiar gate was reached; it stood wide open and there was a great crowd on the side porch with the Bishop's smiling face in the midst of them, and Willard's eyes were so misty and his heart beat so violently he had only a vague impression of being kissed by everybody and slapped on the shoulder by a dozen hands while his hand ached from being so violently shaken.

Of course Aunt Sarah flew out of the house crying hysterically.

"Oh Willard," and she sobbed and hung on his shoulder in true Aunt Sarah style. And of course Hortense mistook her for Aseneth and for the life of her couldn't help the glare of hate from shining in her eyes. But there Aunt Sarah hung, and Willard didn't know for the life of him what to do until the Bishop came up and drawing her away said smilingly,

"You won't leave anything of Willard for his wife, Sarah."

Hortense was intensely relieved. But the Bishop wasn't for Aunt Sarah transferred herself at once to his shoulder, crying out that "Willard was like her own son, her very own son; she couldn't love him better if he was indeed her own, and so being that he could not be her son, which –"

Willard asked someone where Aseneth was, and they told him she was waiting for "them" in the parlor.

With a quick inspiration, he drew Hortense with him and hurried into the hall. The folks instantly closed the hall door, thus leaving the husband and his wives in the privacy of the empty rooms.

As they turned into the main or central hall, a little girl two or three years old with dark curls and a red, pouty mouth stood before them. She looked up silently at them, and as if repeating a well-learned lesson, lisped out, "Papa, Aunty."

"It is the child," quivered Hortense, and catching it to her she crushed the dark curls to her throbbing breast and pressed a hundred kisses on the wondering eyes and rosy mouth.

"It is indeed our child," said her husband after a few moments. She had not noticed, so absorbed had she been, that he had darted into the parlor and was now returned to her side.

"Do I need to introduce you, my two loved wives?" She turned.

Hortense devoured Aseneth with her keen, gray eyes. Her form, her dress, her manner, this at an instant's glance, then she gazed into her eyes. Whoever could look into those lovely, soulful eyes of Aseneth's and be repelled? Hortense looked long, the answering orbs met her own with such sweet pathos, such a longing for her love and sympathy, that not many minutes passed ere she put the child into its father's arms for the first time – and putting her arms around Aseneth and said softly, "You shall be to me what I have never had, a sister."

I am not going to tell you how fast the husband's and father's tears fell over the baby face he held so close to him, nor of the sweet, happy hour that followed. Some things are too sacred for you and me, my dear and patient reader! So we will leave them there in the sweet communion they all had so well and so faithfully earned.

The next event that I have to chronicle is the return to the farm.

Hortense took great delight in showing Aseneth all the pretty and useful things "our Will," as she dubbed her husband at once, had brought in that wonderful trunk. She could not feel jealousy towards Aseneth. Sometimes circumstances hurt her, but never from the moment she sealed her sisterly compact with a kiss did she feel a mean or envious feeling toward her husband's first wife. I wonder indeed who could be jealous of so gentle a soul as Aseneth?

Not until the next Fast-day could Willard and Hortense get married, and things at the farm demanded his attention.

"Willard," said Hortense one evening when they were discussing plans, "I would rather stay up here at the Bishop's. Mrs. Mainwaring, the first wife," she had not yet learned to say Sister or Aunt Mary, "says I am very welcome to stay right here. I shall have a deal of sewing to do, to furnish my room, sheets and table cloths; and I am to learn how to sew carpet rags and patch quilts. One of the girls here, Miss Rhoda, says she will give me pieces enough for a quilt. So I shall have plenty to do."

"I am so glad they want to help you, Patsey. Do just as you think best about the matter. But I shall have to take Aseneth down with me, you know, to look after me," with a somewhat doubtful look to see how she would take the statement.

"Of course. But Will, it will be very lonely to me here alone, with all these strange people, for they are strange even if they are so kind."

"Well, Patsey!"

"Well, if you know, if, well, if, I dared ask Aseneth to let me keep baby Hortense, oh you don't know what a comfort it would be!"

"Ask her, Patsey. It won't do any harm anyway, and very likely she'll say yes."

The result was that, after some very natural hesitation, Aseneth consented to leave the baby, and Hortense was so happy in watching the tiny woman for the next two weeks and in sleeping with her close-clasped in her arms that she forgot to think about her husband being absent from her or with another woman.

Sweet childhood, how great is thy power! To soothe, to comfort, to ennoble and to distract until the weary mother forgets to grieve, forgets all else but thy bright smile!

Part XVI

In the latter part of September that same year Willard came up from the farm bringing Aseneth with him, and the arrangements were all completed for this second wedding between Willard and Hortense. Hortense had remained with the Mainwarings during the summer as she preferred not to go down to the farm until she was once again "legally and lawfully" her dear husband's wife. She had begged the Mainwarings to say nothing about the matter else there would have been a goodly wedding with all the old fashioned accessories of large suppers, a big crowd, and a merry time.

As it was, generous, impulsive Rhoda begged her mother to give her entire charge of the supper, and so while the rest went to witness the ceremony Rhoda robbed nests, wrung the necks of turkeys and chickens, roasted beef, made pies of black and yellow currants, beat up a huge cake, and with pounded sugar and eggs iced it over for the "wedding cake."

Tommy and Aunt Sarah's Helen, who had grown up into a beautiful girl, stayed home to help Rhoda.

The little wedding party were very tired with the long, warm day's exercises, and when, as they stepped into the hall and were at once ushered by Tom into the big, cool, dining room, darkened and thus cleared of flies, the heavily-laden table in the center of the room looked decidedly tempting. The bright glass and white table cloth were set off grandly by the huge white cake in the center decked with wreaths of flowers and with a tall bouquet of scarlet geraniums and green leaves stuck up in the center of the cake. A huge platter with two turkeys faced the Bishop at the head of the table while Willard had to serve the stewed chicken and carve the roast beef as he sat at the foot of the table. A half dozen kinds of vegetables swam in butter or were smothered in cream gravies. And piles of creamy white bread disappeared before the invading hungry host.

Rhoda had given up her room entirely for the summer to Hortense as the latter had preferred to wait in the city until her marriage. And that afternoon when Hortense ran up to her room on an errand, she found, thrown over the bed with a note pinned to it, a lovely blue and white "log cabin" quilt. This was to be her best spread, as white spreads were then unknown luxuries in Utah, and the note told her it had been pieced for her in the winter by the Mainwaring girls after they heard she was coming on in the spring.

Hortense could not prevent her tears falling over this evidence of thoughtful love on the part of people who had never seen her, and after she had carefully dried her eyes she ran downstairs and, searching out

Rhoda and Helen, she took both their hands and with a tearful, "Thank you, girls," she kissed each one on the cheek with quivering lips and a full heart.

Hortense had developed a real and profound love for pretty, winning Rhoda. I do not say that, for some reason of her own, Rhoda, the witch, did not set her plans to accomplish this very end. Howbeit, the two became fast friends, and Hortense took great delight in instructing Rhoda to play on the new organ the Bishop had gotten for his girls.

Insensibly Rhoda's manners as well as those of the rest of the children had grown more refined and gentle under the influences of this cultured woman's presence, while Hortense gained a new insight into the deep, noble wells of self forgetful daily life through her intimacy with this excellent family.

Willard had always spent his Sundays with her, and they both were joyful and faithful attendants at the regular Sabbath meetings.

Hortense grew to love kindly Aunt Mary and to long for a chance to sit down and have a friendly, confidential chat with her as she sometimes did in the long twilights. It was to her that she confided all her past and told her of the heavenly dream which had done so much towards reconciling her to plural marriage.

"But you must also remember, my dear," Aunt Mary had answered the girl, "that plural marriage is not designed only to bring those beautiful unborn spirits here; it is to draw woman out from under the curse that for five or six thousand years has been resting upon her."

This was a new phase of the question. Hortense had followed her husband because she loved him, not because she particularly loved his religion.

"You say you think you can live polygamy because you love Willard and because you are sure you can love Aseneth," went on her wise mentor. "This will never do at all. You must live your religion and be true to your husband and his family even if you don't like one other member of the family but himself. I don't believe any woman should live with and raise children by a man she don't and can't love. But remember, Willard may not always get as good wives as Aseneth."

This was a suggestion unthought of before, and the bare idea sent the blood from the young girl's cheeks to her heart in one big painful surge.

"Oh, do you think 'our Will' will ever marry another woman?" she palpitated.

"Why not? Won't he have as good a right to do so as he had to marry you?" gravely smiling down at the startled eyes.

"There is a current saying among us here," added Aunt Mary, "that the last wife has never been in real polygamy until her husband gets another wife."

Poor Hortense was speechless.

"It seems singular, but there is one thing that can be noted anywhere in the world – good women are far more numerous than are good men. No matter as to other statistics, nor do I stop to say more than this: why this is so we cannot tell you. The cause lies away back in our pre-existence. But let me ask you one question. What is to become of all those extra good women? Is not their longing, yes and their right to become wives and mothers as good as yours or mine? You will note as you live here longer that this is especially the case in this gospel – the scarcity of good men compared to the women. Temporally speaking, it is not so much the right of the man in this Church to have two or more wives; it is the right of the women to have a good and faithful husband."

Verily, Hortense had entered a new world. And it seemed very difficult to drag her feet from the clay which tradition and prejudice had heaped about her feet. However, she was learning.

"Your dream, Hortense, brings to my mind, chiefly because of its being a half-light or one side light, bright though it was, thrown on this important question, a dream of Father Smith's (as the Prophet's father was affectionately called) in Nauvoo. Some new doctrine had been advanced by the Prophet Joseph, and his father did not accept it nor could he understand it at all. So the old man stood facing a huge and forbidding mountain. An angel stood near him and commanded him to ascend the mountain. 'Ah, but I can't,' answered the old gentleman, 'no one could do that, it is so steep.' Instantly he saw one step cut in the side of the mountain. 'Take that step,' said the angel; 'but there is no other' thought the dreamer. However, not daring to disobey, he put his foot on the step, and immediately above was a second step. He took that, and then a third appeared. 'Remember,' said his guide then, 'that you can only take one step at a time'."

"And that is how I have come, Aunt Mary, step by step."

"Then be humble, and you shall go on and on until you reach celestial glory."

These talks did Hortense a world of good, and she was quickly learning the great beauty and worth of the religion she had accepted.

All the Mainwarings and Langs were invited down to the farm one week from Hortense's wedding day, and again were chickens slaughtered and many good things supplied to fill the happy crowd of friends that gathered round the extemporized long table in the central "front room."

I don't think Utah knew a happier man than was Willard that day when he sat at one end of his own table with his wives on either side smiling across the long expanse of dishes and faces at his true and noble friend the Bishop.

Time flew away, and soon Willard had been home a year. His farm prospered under his management, and he was beginning to feel that the promises given to him so long ago were reaching fulfillment.

Aseneth made him the happy father of another baby girl in August of the year following his return.

He was intensely proud of his children and was exceedingly anxious that Hortense should be likewise blessed. But she was not. It was a severe trial to her as well as to him. She wondered how any woman on earth could be happy without children. The spot once filled by her lost boy had never been occupied or healed, and she was painfully sensitive on the subject.

For some reason she took an unaccountable dislike to poor Aunt Sarah. Perhaps it was the lingering trace of that first burst of hatred with which she beheld the poor lady hanging over her husband. And with the suspicion of a watchful wife, she felt sure Aunt Sarah would like Willard to marry pretty Helen, her oldest daughter.

In reality, I don't believe Hortense had a shadow of a nail to hang her suspicions on, but they were just as strong and produced as disagreeable results as if they hung securely on authenticated facts.

Be that as it may, Aunt Sarah could never break down the slight but firm barriers of reserve which persisted in rising between the two. Hortense respected her, watched her every word for its hidden meaning, and while no doubt she often detected the latent meaning so covertly hid from casual ears in the good lady's rapid monologues, still she too often did her profound injustice.

Aunt Sarah's heart was all right, and she was a good, faithful woman, while to most of people she was a dear soul and worthy of the highest honors. But her persistent insincerity which, by most people was variously termed joking, exaggeration, or carelessness, became to the keen-eyed woman watching her, downright dishonesty and trickery.

Thus do we poor womenfolks misunderstand each other. When Hortense gets to heaven, she'll find a good many Aunt Sarahs there, for "Aunt Sarah" is often found in Utah, and is just as deserving of Father's mercy and love as Hortense or women like her who fancy themselves the pint cup in which all should be measured. I wish I could take you clear up to the present day and show you how nobly Aunt Sarah has justified her claims to the respect and admiration of all Saints, but my story now is nearly told and so you must simply take my word for it.

Part XVII

"All the thirty-seven cents and a half gentlemen may now choose a partner for a ladies' tucker dance," sang out the jolly lady floor manager of the grand leap year ball held in the Social Hall in the year of our Lord 1865.

"Isn't that Rhoda Mainwaring leading Willard on for this dance?" I asked Hortense as I tried to squint with my shortsighted eyes at the rapidly filling floor.

"That's our Will leading Rhoda Gibbs on for this dance; it's gentlemen's choice, this dance, as you say out here," and the speaker laughed softly, albeit I fancied with a tiny catch in the voice so bravely gay.

"Patsey Gibbs!" I ejaculated, breathless with surprise. "What do you mean?"

"I mean that Rhoda Mainwaring is now Rhoda Gibbs." The voice was quite steady now, and if the lips trembled a little, the clear eyes met mine without a suspicion of tears or anger. Just then a tiny bundle of flannels on a neighboring window seat gave unmistakable signs of life and hunger, and Hortense ran to it with a pretty, half-startled mother cry in her throat, and I was left to my own reflections on this last and most astounding piece of news.

I sat watching the dancers and unconsciously noticed the tasteful decorations arranged by careful hands, the large windows curtained with somebody's treasured lace curtains, the spaces in between the windows filled with fearful and wonderful pictures, likewise borrowed for the occasion; the flag at the further end of the hall twined in graceful folds above the musician's heads. On the stage where I sat, the bright, home-made carpet added a pleasant look to the resting place of mothers, weary fathers and gossipy matrons. Tables here and there were strewn with borrowed albums, small and queer, but very precious in those days, with an occasional set of stereoscopic view which were eagerly sought for by young and old. Arm chairs in the front of the stage held in their generous home-made embraces the venerable old who came to enjoy by "looking on," as well as the honored Presidency who sometimes sought rest from the dance.

From the basement came to my nose the smell of roasting chickens, fried sausages, and all the thousand and one odors of a feast of the olden time that made a well person far hungrier by their appetizing presence but were apt to spoil the taste of a dyspeptic or over-sensitive person. Assuredly Willard and Rhoda made a charming picture as they gracefully swung and balanced, now separated by the "Tucker," now together with a gleeful clasp of hands. Neither Aseneth with her grey eyes, pale skin and rather neutral tinted ensemble, nor Hortense, so brilliant and dark in her magnificent beauty made the pleasing contrast to Willard's own dark, if handsome, features that this rosy-cheeked, blue-eyed, winsome Rhoda Mainwaring – Gibbs, I beg your pardon Mrs. Rhoda – did as they danced and laughed together.

Aseneth and Hortense wore their red merino dresses alike in color and simple style, and both were fair to look upon, while Rhoda's new blue delaine flounced to the top of her skirt gave her a flying, cloud-like look that was an added attraction to the pretty figure. Verily Willard Gibbs was a fortunate man.

While I sat thinking about this singular piece of news that had been imparted to me by Hortense, she came up to me with her baby in her arms and said, "Come down into the dressing room, Aunty, and I will tell you all about it."

I willingly complied, and we found ourselves alone in the dense forest of cloaks, wraps and bundles.

"Isn't he lovely?" Hortense asked me for the twentieth time that evening, holding up to my gaze a very red faced baby. I hasted to assure her of my continued allegiance to his Majesty, and begged her to begin her tale, for we were not sure of our solitude two minutes together.

"You know, dear Aunty, something of my terrible suffering at the time I lost my little boy in Virginia; and yet the half could not be told. It was all right, though; I admitted that when Oscar died and bore such a faithful testimony of my condition as Willard's wife. I consented to come here as Will's second wife, and you with your Mormon training can hardly guess what that cost me; but I overcame that. Aseneth is such a dear, good girl that it's not at all difficult to love her and be generous to her. But one awful day Aunt Mary suggested to me the possibility of Will's taking another wife after me. I say it was an awful day, for I felt all the influences of this evil world let loose in my mind. Why should he do so, I asked myself and him a thousand useless times. It seemed as if my body would be worn out with the terrible conflict going on in my soul; and I could also see Will was suffering almost as much as I was. Then, came the frightful suspicion that Aunt Sarah was trying to inveigle Will into marrying her daughter Helen. I disliked Aunt Sarah before, but that made me have feelings towards her that were positively wicked. As for Helen, her name, her face, or her voice was enough to send me foaming and raging into my room. I did not tell Will about Helen, for after all I was ashamed to confess all my feelings. I am glad I did not go too far, for I believe I would have lost my soul and done some rash act if I had gone many steps further. God was good to me, wretched as I was.

One day Will told me that he had, after much study and prayer, decided to ask some girl to marry him. It all seemed so little like religion and so much like something bad that I did what I never have done in my life. I stooped to low language and vile recriminations. I never saw Will so angry in my life. He said in a low, strained voice, "Hortense, if that is what you think of me and my actions, I cannot in justice to myself look upon you as my wife. It will be far better for us to live apart."

"And so it was. For months we lived in the same house, but when we were alone, he never spoke one word to me nor acted as if he knew I were in the house. Aseneth suspected something was wrong, but like the wise girl she is, she did not interfere. Will seemed to abandon all thought of ever getting another wife, and in place of the terrible fire that I had been burning in my veins for months, a slow, silent misery seemed to envelop me as with a veil. I could not eat much, and my only comfort was the long, dreamless sleeps that mercifully came and blotted out memory and woe."

"One night I had a dream. When I awoke in the morning, I was conscious that I had dreamed a dream that I ought to remember. And I lay still for quite a while trying to remember what it was. Suddenly I caught sight of my little boy's framed photograph which hangs near my bed, and the whole dream came as by a flash. I found myself in my dream in the same low, clay valley I had seen in my vision in Virginia; and the clouds were very dark and threatening overhead. I was plodding along, over my ankles in the loathsome mud. As I stumbled along, I muttered, 'Oh God, what does this mean?' Gradually a rift was made in the clouds hanging so low over me, and away up in the blue of space I saw plainer and plainer the face of my boy with two little faces on each side of him. He looked so lovely and yet so sadly reproachful that my soul groaned within me. Then as their faces grew fainter with their swift uprising, I saw a rosebud falling, falling until it fluttered at my feet. I picked it up and as I held it to my lips I awoke, or at least that was the end of my dream."

"The lesson bore its fruit. I went to my husband, made a full confession of all that had troubled me, and asked him to forgive the cruel words I had uttered. He was full of sympathy and love, and after a long conversation I found out that the only way to conquer trials is to want to conquer them, and then to pray always for strength to do so. I discovered, too, that my suspicions were not without foundation; at least Willard had resolved to ask Helen Mainwaring to be his wife. It was weeks before I could say to him go ahead and God bless you. He did not attempt to get her consent, though, till I said this, of that I am sure. And it cost me many a severe struggle to say it, but say it I did. Then he went about his business."

"Now came over me a longing for children that was exquisite pain in its intensity. I suffered agony in seeing the evident hopes of other women becoming mothers. To know that any of my friends had given birth to a child caused me to suffer such distress as falls to the lot of many a childless woman. I would weep all night upon hearing such news, and I could not even bring myself to look upon the child. It came to me one day that I was a very ungrateful and very unsatisfactory child to my heavenly Father. I heard a sermon preached by Brother Heber C. Kimball that showed me my true position. Here I was on the earth to earn a glorious salvation in the next world, and all the time I was spending my whole time and strength in uselessly bemoaning my fate. I was not only wasting time and strength, but I was making many others miserable by my unreasonable rebellion against the decrees of the Almighty. He said in the same sermon that it depended upon ourselves greatly the sort of blessings we had. I went home resolved to do differently. If it depended upon myself as to my blessings, I should do all I could to put myself in the way of having the desire of my heart.

A long interruption here stopped Hortense, and when we were again at peace, she resumed.

"With all my soul I desired children; and night after night I prayed to God to grant me this prayer. A year passed away, and one day Will came home and that night he told Aseneth and me that he had asked Helen Mainwaring to marry him and she had refused. Not very politely either. However, I was not as sorry for this refusal as I ought to have been, and I am afraid I said in my own soul, 'Thank the Lord for that'!"

"But it was gradually impressed upon my mind that if my husband would get another wife that I should have the desire of my heart realized. So, having that faith, I began to feel willing and at last even anxious for Will to get a third wife. I actually began to pray that he might be successful in finding a good girl to share our home and love, so sure was I that then would I have my heart's desire. Again he sought a girl's consent; this time it was one of Aseneth's sisters, but again he was refused. This time I was as sorry as Aseneth, and told them both so. I believe the Lord saw I was honest, and isn't it rather funny," she bent low to my ear and whispered, "in ten months from that time, this dear little cherub came to me from those realms of light. And oh, don't you think I am paid a thousand times over for what I have sacrificed?"

"Yes," I say. "But what about Rhoda?"

"Is this here precinct sacred to women gossipers alone?" asks a merry voice at the door, and Tom's freckled, jolly face peeps in the doorway.

"Oh, Tom," says Hortense in a relieved voice, "you come in and tell Aunty about Will and Rhoda. She hasn't heard a word about it till tonight."

"Well, if you want to know the ins and outs of it I am just the fellow that can give 'em to you. Of course, you know, Aunty, about Rhoda's putting up that chicken bone over the door the very first day Willard ever came to our house, and how Will caught her in his arms and gave her a rousing smack. Oh my!" and the young man laid back and laughed uproariously, "it just upsets me every time I think of Rhoda's red face when she dashed back into the house. Well, you see, I had given up teasing our Rhoda about Will for years, and I never imagined that she ever did care a red cent about him, although I kinder fancied that Will liked Rhoda."

"I didn't," murmured Hortense, softly but not angrily.

"One day last week I came home in the middle of the forenoon to get something for father, and I accidentally stepped into the front hall. Who should I see perched upon a high chair, reaching up to the top of the front door but her high and mighty ladyship, Rhoda."

"'See here,' I said, 'what on earth are you doing there, miss'?"

"She looked ready to eat me up, and sassed back, 'Go away Thomas Mainwaring, and for once, mind your own business and let me alone'."

"'Whew!' I said, 'What are you doing that you are so ashamed of?' All of a sudden it popped into my head that this was another wishbone, and I hollered out, 'You needn't color so high, miss, nor bother to watch for your intended, for Johnny Lawson is up in the canyon, Harry Wilmont is down in Fillmore, and as for Willard Gibbs –"

"'Who takes my name in vain?' said Willard as he pushed open the front door and thus gave Miss Rhoda a tumble, helter, skelter, right into his arms for the second time. I just thought I should have died a laughing. But Rhoda, like any girl, began to bawl. Willard set her on her feet, and then, looking at me pretty sternlike, he asked, 'Thomas, I expect you to give me an explanation of this affair. What are you laughing at? I should think you would be ashamed to see your sister suffering on your account."

"Well I didn't see any reason to be ashamed. She was the one to feel cheap, but I just turned in and told him the story of the first wishbone, which it seems, he had never heard, and then told him how I had caught her a second time at it. He wasn't looking at me while I talked, but stood holding Rhoda's arm so she shouldn't run away, and when I got through, he just kinder whispered stern like, high tragedy you know, 'Miss Rhoda, will you be my dear little wife?'"

"What did you say then," I asked, for Tom's words were far more unkindly than his tone or his heart, and I knew he had been touched in spite of himself. Rhoda had slipped into the dressing room while we talked and now sat at Hortense's feet, cooing and purring at the baby which she had taken in her arms.

"Need you ask what Tom would say, when you know how manly he thinks it is to be slangy and vulgar," asked Rhoda, with a reproachful glance up at her laughing brother, "He ejaculated, 'Gosh?' and then fled like the wind for the back door."

"Well, it did seem spoiling the very best joke I ever knew. I was plum disgusted," said blunt Tom.

"Oh, Thomas, I didn't think you would treat so sacred a subject as this so lightly," said Hortense sadly. "To me it is a sacrilege to talk so flippantly about such things." The words were keen, but the tone was so kindly that the reproof only made Tom a little thoughtful.

"It was a sacred thing to me, dear Aunty," said Rhoda. "I can assure you I felt very solemn as the meaning of Will's words came to me. Here for years I had dreamed about such a thing, and now that it had come, it seemed too bad to have it made so commonplace by that horrid Tom. But my past experience had taught me that I could not treat Willard with any coquetry, so after asking him some questions and telling him that I did not want to go into his family unless both girls were willing, I said the fateful yes." And the dear little girl, so innocent and girlish in spite of her twenty-five years, buried her face in the baby's blanket folds to conceal her blushes.

"My dear friend," said Hortense to Rhoda in her firm, serious way, "if I could have had my choice out of the whole world, I would have chosen you for Will's third wife for I know you are a good and true and above all of a loving and forgiving disposition."

"Is this a council of war?" asked the husband of these three girls as he came in with Aseneth. They stood over Hortense and she looked up and answered softly, "No dear, it is a council of love."

"Blessed are good wives. And lucky is the man who has his quiver full of 'em," quoted Tom recklessly.

"Some more talk about the only baby that ever was born on the earth," purred Aunt Sarah as she glided into the room in search of someone. "I do declare, it beats all how young mothers think their own particular crow is the whitest. Tsa-tsa-tsa," she chirruped to the blinking bundle in Rhoda's lap. "It seems quite a pretty little thing, but it looks kind o' puny and rickety, don't it? Maybe it's because its parents were born where folks eat so much pork; or else it's like lots of other babies whose father has been a man of the world. What on earth are you glaring at me for, Rhoda? I haven't said anything, only that Willard did not have the privilege of being born in Utah. No harm in that, I hope. What makes you all so silent for, anyway? And Rhoda's face is more blushing than usual, and goodness knows that is unnecessary," laughing at her own pleasantry. "Have you been telling Aunty here, Rhoda, how many years you were trying to catch Willard and how uncommonly lucky your sly little wishbones were at helping you out? Law me, I could have told Will any time if he had only asked me how Rhoda would have jumped at the chance of having him, but he didn't ask me. I knew how it was when he sparked Aseneth because he thought he couldn't get Rhody, but as I said he wouldn't take the trouble to ask my advice. It beats all how some women will run after a man, and even leave a home of wealth and ease to come out here to poverty and privation when other girls won't so much as look at a man. Now, there's my Helen, it just wears me out trying to keep track of her offers. You may be sure, she has not only refused common men but the big bugs have tried it in vain. Dear me, sometimes I am worn right out with the men who are always running after her. She is too smart for common men; she is watching for the best. But I do declare, it just almost makes me cry to see how terribly some of her cast-off beaus feel. If all my girls try me in this way as she does, I think I shall have to give up the whole business into the Bishop's hands," and the lady wiped her eyes as if in distress.

"It is better to live on the roof with boiled carrots than to be in the house with a bawling martyr," softly murmured Tom.

"Come, come, come, you folks, do you know I have been looking all over the hall for you. Everyone else has gone down to supper long ago. What are you about?" The worthy Bishop stood in the doorway with Aunts Mary and Fanny.

"Some of us are comparing notes," answers Hortense.

"And some a-counting votes," says Aunt Sarah.

"One is finding motes the size of an ax handle," finishes Tom.

The Bishop is already leading the way with his wives. He turns around to say to Willard, "It must be quite a testimony to you, Brother Willard, the way in which you and yours have been brought up from tribulation to the light and glory of the gospel. God loves the pure in heart."

Willard has Aseneth on his arm, but stops short to say to the two who follow close behind, their arms in girlish fashion clasped about each other, "Say girls, I think I am the most blessed man in all this universe. Do you believe it?"

And then they all find a place at one of the huge, well-filled tables, while Hortense whispered to Rhoda, "Dear, this is not a bad wedding supper, is it?"

You see, that was Willard's and Rhoda's wedding day.

THE END

Homespun

Made in the USA
San Bernardino, CA
05 October 2018